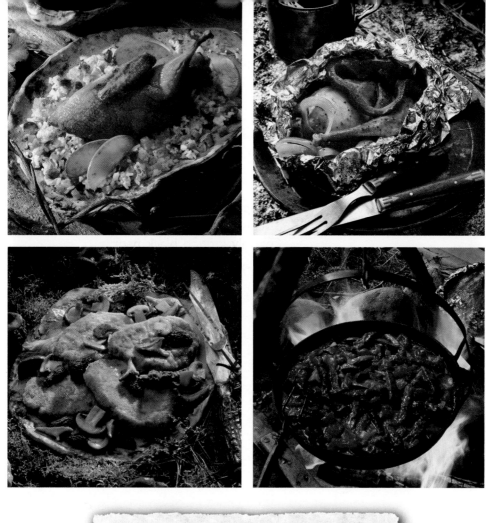

HUNTING REWARDS

Members' Game Recipes

NORTH★AMERICAN★HUNTING★CLUB

Minnetonka, Minnesota

Hunting Rewards: Members' Game Recipes

Mike Vail *Vice President, Product and Business Development*

Tom Carpenter *Director of Book Development*

Dan Kennedy *Book Production Manager*

Jen Guinea *Book Development Coordinator*

Shari Gross *Book Development Assistant*

Teresa Marrone *Editor*

BatScanner Productions, Inc. *Book Design and Production*

Bill Lindner Photography *Photography*
Abigail Wyckoff *Prop and Food Stylist*
Susan Telleen *Assistant Food Stylist*
Pete Cozad *Assistant Photographer*

Additional photography
Dan Kennedy *(page 99)*
Bill Marchel *(pages 6-7, 32-33, 72-73, 94-95, 114-115, 134-135)*
Stan Osolinski, The Green Agency *(pages 48-49)*
Dusan Smetana, The Green Agency *(page 155)*
Ron Spomer *(pages 4-5, 118, 124, 128, 130)*
Bill Vaznis, The Green Agency *(page 148)*
Brandon Williamson *(page 112)*
Ed Sutton *Artwork (page 82)*

Special thanks to: Adam DeChaine, Paul DeChaine, Pete DeChaine, Ryan DeChaine, Bob Ehli, Brook Martin, Monte and Kelly Strand, Jim Reimers, Jason Lund and Mike Hehner.

The North American Hunting Club proudly presents this special edition cookbook that includes the personal favorites of your fellow Members. Each recipe has been screened by a cooking professional and edited for clarity. However, we are not able to kitchen-test these recipes and cannot guarantee their outcome or your safety in their preparation or consumption. Please be advised that any recipes that require the use of dangerous equipment (such as pressure cookers) or potentially unsafe procedures (such as marinating, canning or pickling) should be used with caution and safe, healthy practices.

ISBN 1-58159-109-8

1 2 3 4 5 6 7 8 / 02 01 00

North American Hunting Club
12301 Whitewater Drive
Minnetonka, MN 55343

TABLE of CONTENTS

INTRODUCTION

Hunting rewards come in two forms.

First, hunting makes memories—feelings and pictures that reside in our minds and let us re-live a hunt whenever we want or need to. When you can't actually be out in the field, recalling a good hunt is about as close as you can get to the real thing.

But hunting also produces another reward—some of the finest eating you will find on this earth. While most North American Hunting Club members aren't out hunting for subsistence, it's still true that game meat forms a staple of the family diet for many

of us: venison from whitetails to muleys to antelope, elk and moose; upland birds of all descriptions; small game such as rabbits and squirrels; and ducks from dabblers to divers.

Eating game—that other fruit of our hunting efforts—is as much a part of the hunt as watching the sun rise, breathing a little faster and better, feeling alive on all fronts, and yes, even pulling the trigger or releasing the arrow.

So we present you with *Hunting Rewards*. Our hope is that the pictures here will take you out to forest, field, swamp, marsh, mountain, hill, prairie, thicket and river-

bottom, and help you recall some of your fondest hunting memories. We also want to help you make the most of that other hunting reward—great game meat—with the 200-plus recipes included.

North American Hunting Club members were kind enough to share these jewels, their very favorite game dishes. You owe it to the game you bring home to do it justice in the kitchen. These recipes are guaranteed to do the job for you, in that regard.

Why do you hunt so hard every year? Like other North American Hunting Club members, myself included, you've probably spent a good chunk of your lifetime "out there" looking for the answers. Of course, that's just the way we like it!

As you continue your search—as I will—let these recipes help you make the most of the delicious game meat you bring home.

Tom Carpenter
*Editor—North American
Hunting Club Books*

VENISON

'After the Hunt' Venison Stew

¼ cup flour
14x20-inch oven roasting bag
1½ tsp. salt
1 tsp. dry mustard
½ tsp. chili powder
¼ tsp. pepper
¼ cup chili sauce
2 T. vinegar
1 T. honey

2 tsp. Worcestershire sauce
3 lbs. venison stew meat, cut into cubes
1 (16-oz.) can tomatoes, cut up
1 large onion, cut into ¾-inch pieces
1 green bell pepper, cut into ¾-inch pieces
2 cups diagonally sliced carrots
2 cups potato chunks
1 cup frozen peas, thawed

Add flour to oven roasting bag and shake well. Place bag in 13x9x2-inch baking dish. Add salt, mustard, chili powder, pepper, chili sauce, vinegar, honey and Worcestershire sauce; turn bag to mix. Add remaining ingredients; turn bag to mix. Seal bag with provided tie. Make 4 to 6 half-inch slits in the top of the bag. Bake at 325°F for 2½ hours, or until venison is fork-tender.

If you prefer, omit potatoes and serve stew over egg noodles. Or make a pot pie by placing cooked stew into a prepared pie crust, topping with a second crust and baking at 400°F for 30 to 40 minutes.

Ron and Mary Lange
Marquette, WI

Uncle Pete's Venison Italiano

10 lbs. venison stew meat, trimmed and
    cut into ¾-inch cubes
¾ cup cooking oil
9 cloves garlic
14 fresh parsley sprigs, chopped
¼ cup bay leaves, chopped
5 hot cherry peppers, chopped

1 T. sugar
1 tsp. salt
1 tsp. black pepper
1 large can crushed tomatoes
1 (8-oz.) can tomato paste
½ cup hot cherry pepper juice, *optional*

Spray bottom of pressure cooker with nonstick spray. Add venison and cook over medium heat, stirring occasionally, until browned on all sides. Drain and discard liquid from pressure cooker. Add remaining ingredients except crushed tomatoes, tomato paste and hot pepper juice. Sauté for approximately 15 minutes. Add remaining ingredients, then put lid on and bring to pressure. Cook for about 45 minutes. Make sure cooker pressure drops to safe level before removing lid. Serve as a main meal, or in Italian rolls as sandwiches. This recipe can be cooked ahead and frozen. Potatoes, sweet peppers and other vegetables can be added if desired.

Richard Denton
Auburn, IL

Venison Shepherd's Pie

4 T. butter, divided (half of a stick)
2 medium onions, chopped
3 cups diced or chopped cooked venison
1 T. chopped basil
Salt and pepper
½ cup beef broth
3 cups mashed potatoes
1 egg, lightly beaten

In heavy skillet, melt 3 tablespoons of the butter. Add onions and sauté for 3 to 4 minutes. Add venison, basil, and salt and pepper to taste. Cook for 5 minutes, stirring occasionally. Add beef broth and simmer for 5 minutes. Transfer meat mixture to 9-inch pie plate. Cover meat with mashed potatoes. Dot potatoes with remaining 1 tablespoon butter, and brush with beaten egg. Bake at 350°F for 15 minutes, or until golden brown.

Ken Colgan
Flushing, NY

Barbecued Deer Ham

1 deer ham
1 (16-oz.) pkg. bacon
1 large oven roasting bag
2 cups barbecue sauce
½ cup honey
Salt and pepper

Make wide slits in the ham, cutting as deeply as possible. Fill slits with bacon, then place ham in oven roasting bag. In mixing bowl, blend together barbecue sauce, honey, and salt and pepper to taste. Pour sauce mixture over meat. Close and seal bag, then cut several slits in top of bag. Bake at 325°F for 1 hour. Reduce oven to 225°F and continue cooking overnight.

Sonny Worsham
Hendersonville, NC

Crock Pot Venison & Mushrooms

3 lbs. venison, cut into 1-inch cubes
¾ cup red cooking wine
1 (1½-oz.) pkg. dry onion soup mix
1 (10¾-oz.) can golden mushroom soup
1 (10¾-oz.) can cream of mushroom soup
1 to 3 cups fresh or canned mushroom slices
Hot cooked noodles, rice or potatoes

Combine all ingredients except noodles in slow cooker and stir well. Cover and cook on low for 10 to 12 hours, then increase heat to high and cook for 1 hour longer. Serve over noodles, rice or potatoes. For some added zing, top with sour cream before serving. You may also use drained, canned venison in place of the cubes.

Brent Bacon
Lewisburg, PA

Venison Tenderloin

1 whole venison tenderloin
5 slices bacon
Butter
1 onion, sliced
Worcestershire sauce

As soon as the deer is hung up and cooling, remove the tenderloin by inserting the blade along the backbone while pulling the meat away with your left hand. Trim all silverskin and fat from tenderloin. Cut into small steaks. Wrap in bacon and sauté in butter with sliced onion and Worcestershire sauce. Serve with a toothpick.

Paul J. Woychik
Arcadia, WI

Venison Liver & Bacon

2 lbs. deer liver, sliced ½ inch thick
Milk
8 slices bacon
½ cup flour
1 tsp. salt
½ tsp. pepper
1 stick butter or margarine (8 T.)

Soak liver slices in milk overnight in refrigerator. Drain and pat dry, discarding milk. In skillet, cook bacon until crisp over low heat. Drain bacon; set aside and keep warm. In shallow dish, combine flour, salt and pepper. Roll liver slices in flour mixture. In heavy skillet, melt butter over high heat. Add liver slices and cook until lightly browned on both sides, about 5 minutes per side. Serve liver topped with bacon slices.

Clete Bellin
Forestville, WI

Hunter-Style Venison Stew

3 to 4 lbs. choice venison
2 T. vegetable shortening
2 lemons, well washed
1 slice smoked ham, cubed
4 cloves garlic, sliced
1 large white onion, sliced
2 bay leaves
1 T. ground thyme
1 tsp. ground cumin
1 tsp. ground sage
1 tsp. Lawry's seasoned salt

1 tsp. plain salt
1 tsp. black pepper
2 (10½-oz.) cans consommé
2 beef bouillon cubes
1½ cups fresh mushrooms, sliced
6 green onions, chopped
1 T. dried parsley flakes
2 T. flour
2 cups dry white wine
Brown toast or hot cooked rice

Cut venison into ¾-inch cubes and brown in shortening in large skillet. While the venison is browning, carefully cut the yellow part of the peels from the lemon in very thin slices; set peels and lemons aside. When venison is browned, add lemon peels, ham, garlic, white onion, bay leaves, thyme, cumin, sage, seasoned salt, plain salt and pepper to skillet. Stir well, then simmer for 20 minutes.

Pour consommé into slow cooker. Cut the 2 reserved lemons in half and squeeze juice into slow cooker through a sieve to strain out seeds; discard lemons. Add bouillon cubes, mushrooms, green onions and parsley flakes. Use slotted spoon to transfer venison and other ingredients from skillet to slow cooker. Sprinkle flour over drippings in skillet and cook, stirring constantly, until flour browns and thickens. Add wine to skillet and cook, stirring constantly, until wine mixture has thickened slightly. Pour wine mixture into slow cooker. Add water to just cover all ingredients, and stir well. Cover and cook on low for 3 to 4 hours. Serve with brown toast or over rice.

Variation: Use a large pot such as a Dutch oven instead of the slow cooker. Cook on the stovetop over low heat for 1 to 2 hours. Moose or elk meat may also be substituted for venison.

This recipe is a Thanksgiving and Christmas tradition on both sides of my family. I started with the basic recipe 28 years ago and think this is the perfected version. Haven't changed it in over 15 years now. I know this will be a big hit to any big-game hunter. Many a so-called "I won't eat deer meat" person has fallen prey to this feast.

T.J. McWhorter
Bowdon, GA

Pan-Seared Venison Filets
with Balsamic Cream Sauce

Pan-Seared Venison Filets with Balsamic Cream Sauce

1 lb. venison backstrap, cut into 4 filets
  approx. 2 inches thick
⅔ cup plus 2 T. balsamic vinegar, divided
2 T. olive oil, divided

1 T. coarse sea salt
1 cup heavy cream
½ tsp. crumbled dried tarragon
2 tsp. multicolored peppercorns

Moisten venison filets with 2 tablespoons of the vinegar and let rest up to 30 minutes. Use a paper towel to rub a tablespoon of the olive oil into a warm, medium cast-iron skillet. Add salt to skillet and rub with same paper towel. Discard salt. Add the second tablespoon of the oil to skillet and place over medium-high heat. When skillet is hot, add filets and sear on both sides, then continue cooking until filets are not quite desired doneness, turning as needed. Transfer filets to warm plate; cover loosely and set aside.

Add remaining ⅔ cup vinegar to hot skillet, scraping to loosen any browned bits. Cook over high heat until vinegar is reduced to about 3 tablespoons. Add cream, tarragon and peppercorns to skillet and continue cooking until liquid is reduced to about half volume. Reduce heat to simmer and return filets to skillet. Turn filets several times to warm and coat with sauce. Transfer filets to heated serving platter. Pour sauce into gravy boat, straining to remove peppercorns and tarragon if desired. Serve immediately.

Note: Venison filets are best served medium-rare; avoid cooking to well-done. Not only is this a very special main course for favorite guests, this is also a magnificent Valentine's Day dinner. Pair it up with wild rice, fresh green beans with slivered toasted almonds, a dry red wine, and a chocolate dessert.

C.T. Rybka
Port Tobacco, MD

Kenny's Juniper Berry Tenderloin

½ cup crushed juniper berries
¼ cup crushed peppercorns
2 venison tenderloins, 1 to 1½ lbs.
2 T. olive oil
1½ cups good red wine

2 cups sliced mushrooms such as portobello,
  chanterelle, morels etc.
Flour blended with cold water
3 T. unsalted butter

Combine juniper berries and peppercorns on plate. Roll venison in berry mixture to coat evenly on all sides. Heat oil in large cast-iron skillet until it just begins smoking. Sear venison on all sides. Transfer skillet to 400°F oven and cook for 10 to 12 minutes. Remove skillet from oven. Transfer meat to warm plate; cover loosely and set aside. Deglaze skillet with wine, stirring to loosen any browned bits. Add mushrooms and cook for 10 to 15 minutes, until mushrooms are tender. Thicken wine sauce with a little flour slurry. Add butter, a tablespoon at a time, stirring until each tablespoon is dissolved before adding the next. When sauce is finished, slice meat and spoon sauce over meat.

Ken Colgan
Flushing, NY

Deer Liver on a Stick

Deer liver
Slab bacon
Onion, quartered and sliced ¼ inch thick
Salt and pepper
Vegetable oil or shortening

Cut liver into pieces that are 1½ × 1½ × ½ inch. Cut bacon into ¼-inch-thick slices, then cut slices into 1½-inch squares. Spear liver, bacon and onions on skewers, alternating in order given, until each skewer is filled for about 6 inches. Place skewers on baking sheet or plate and sprinkle top side with salt and pepper.

Heat ½ inch oil in large skillet over medium heat. Lay skewers in skillet, seasoned side up, and cook until browned on bottom side, checking frequently to avoid burning the bottom side. When bottom side is browned, turn skewers, sprinkle with salt and pepper, and cook until second side is browned. Simple but good!

John Katinas
Bellerose, NY

Venison Tongue Sandwich Spread

Venison tongue
Chopped onion
Mayonnaise

Boil tongue in water to cover until tender, about 1 hour. Cool tongue and run through meat grinder. Add chopped onion to taste, and enough mayonnaise to make it spread easily.

E.B. Flener
Cromwell, KY

Hunter's Booya

6 lbs. venison
4 wild ducks, cut into halves
2 lbs. cubed pork
2½ lbs. soup bones
4 large onions, sliced
2 cups fresh parsley sprigs
½ cup dry lima beans
½ cup dry split peas
¼ cup salt
2 T. pepper
2 T. garlic salt
1 T. crumbled dried basil leaves
1 T. crumbled dried oregano leaves
1 tsp. crumbled dried savory leaves

In very large kettle, combine all above ingredients. Heat to boiling. Reduce heat, cover and simmer 4 to 5 hours, or until meat is tender. Remove meat and bones from kettle and set aside to cool slightly. Pull meat from bones and cut meat into cubes; discard bones. Skim fat from stock and return meat to kettle.

3 cups diced carrots
3 cups diced celery
1 large head red cabbage, coarsely chopped
1 cup diced rutabaga
1 cup diced green bell pepper

After returning boned meat to kettle, add all above ingredients. Cover and simmer for 1 hour.

3 (28-oz.) cans tomatoes, undrained
3 (15½-oz.) cans cut green beans, undrained
2 (10-oz.) pkgs. frozen peas
2 (10-oz.) pkgs. frozen whole-kernel corn

After simmering fresh vegetables for an hour, add all above ingredients. Cover and simmer for 1 hour longer. Serves 30 to 35 generously.

Paul J. Woychik
Arcadia, WI

Crooked Chimney Camp
High-Heart-in-the-Hole Sandwich

1 deer heart, thinly sliced
1 lb. fresh mushrooms, thinly sliced
1 medium onion, thinly sliced
1 tsp. minced garlic

2 T. butter
2 hoagy buns, split into halves
Sliced Swiss cheese
A-1 Sweet & Tangy sauce, *optional*

In large skillet, sauté heart, mushrooms, onion and garlic in butter over medium heat until heart is medium-rare to medium doneness (do not overcook). Arrange buns, open-faced, on baking sheet. Divide heart mixture evenly between buns; top with sliced Swiss cheese. Bake at 350°F until cheese melts. Serve open-faced, with A-1 sauce if desired.

This is a good snack during a late-night card game. Dealer calls high heart in the hole, and whoever has it has to make the sandwiches.

Mark Starszak
Saukville, WI

Venison Swiss Steak for Two

2 T. flour
¾ tsp. salt, divided
¼ tsp. pepper
¾ lb. boneless venison steak, about ½ inch thick

1 T. vegetable oil
1 (8-oz.) can stewed tomatoes
1 medium green bell pepper, sliced
1 medium onion, sliced

In resealable plastic bag, combine flour, ¼ teaspoon of the salt, and the pepper; shake to mix. Add steak and shake to coat. In large skillet, brown steak in oil over medium heat. Add tomatoes; cover and simmer for 30 minutes. Add bell pepper, onion and remaining ½ teaspoon salt. Cover and simmer until meat is tender, 20 to 30 minutes longer.

Robert Gailey
Nezperce, ID

Laurie's Venison Stroganoff

1½ lbs. boneless venison steak or chops
1 stick butter (8 T.), divided
1 cup wine or beer
½ cup ketchup
2 T. Italian seasoning blend
1 T. pepper
1 T. Miracle Blend salt or 1½ tsp. plain salt
4 ribs celery, sliced
1 medium onion, chopped
1½ cups fresh mushrooms, sliced,
   or 2 (8-oz.) cans sliced mushrooms
3 T. cornstarch blended with 1 cup cold water
1 to 1½ cups sour cream
Hot cooked rice or pasta

Cut venison in small, bite-sized pieces, trimming away all fat. Melt 4 tablespoons butter in large skillet and brown venison lightly on one side. Turn meat and add wine, ketchup, Italian seasoning, pepper and salt blend. Cook over medium heat, stirring occasionally, for about 30 minutes, or until wine mixture has reduced to about half of original volume. While meat cooks, sauté celery, onion and mushrooms in remaining 4 tablespoons butter in a separate skillet until tender-crisp; remove from heat and set aside.

When wine has reduced to about half-volume, add cornstarch slurry, stirring constantly. Cook, stirring frequently, until sauce thickens, about 10 minutes. Stir in cooked mushroom mixture, then gently stir in sour cream and heat briefly (do not boil). Serve with rice or pasta.

Norm Maxwell
Manchester, MI

Impatient Butcher's Treats

Whipped sweet cream butter
6 venison tenderloin steaks, ⅛ to ¼ inch thick
Coarsely ground black pepper
¼ to ½ tsp. ground cayenne pepper

For appetizers: In skillet, melt butter over low heat, then add steaks and peppers. Simmer for about 5 minutes, then turn and continue simmering until meat no longer runs pink. Increase heat to high for 1 to 2 minutes, and brown both sides. Transfer meat to bowl; top with skillet juices.

For a meal: Use butterflied tenderloin steaks. Cook as directed above, then transfer meat to warmed plate. Thicken pan juices with cornstarch blended with milk or wine to make gravy. Serve over rice.

Tim Lepley
St. Albans, WV

Venison Mincemeat Pie Filling

Part One:
2 lbs. cooked venison of any kind
½ lb. beef suet (from the butcher)
5 lbs. pared apples, diced small
3 lbs. raisins
1 lb. currents
2 cups brown sugar
1 quart sweet apple cider, plus additional
   if needed
1 cup meat stock
1 T. salt

Part Two:
1 small orange, well washed
1 small lemon, well washed
1 quart grape juice
1 cup molasses
¾ cup vinegar
2 tsp. ground allspice
2 tsp. ground cloves
2 tsp. nutmeg
2 tsp. cinnamon
1 tsp. mace
½ tsp. pepper

Grind venison and suet through meat grinder, using fine grinding plate. Combine venison mixture and all remaining ingredients from Part One in large kettle (preferably nonaluminum) and heat to boiling. Reduce heat and simmer at least 1 hour, stirring occasionally; add more cider if needed.

Grind orange and lemon, including peels, through fine meat grinding plate. Add ground orange and lemon, along with all remaining ingredients from Part Two, to cooked mixture from Part One. Heat to boiling. Reduce heat and simmer for 30 to 60 minutes, until correct pie filling consistency is reached. Pack while hot into hot sterilized canning jars (approximately 6) and seal tight. Process in hot-water canning bath, following standard canning procedures, for 30 minutes. Instead of canning, you may pack into airtight containers and freeze. It takes about 3 cups of filling to make a 9-inch pie.

Note: We use this recipe to make mincemeat pies year-round. It was developed by my mother, Alleen Thompson, who is 88 and still baking all the family pies. We like the results so much, we keep a copy of the recipe in the safe beside the deed to the farm. Traditionally, we use neck meat in the recipe. I have used a number of different species including bear, antelope and bighorn, and they have all worked well.

John Thompson
Evergreen, CO

Chicken-Fried Venison Steak

2 lbs. boneless venison steak (4 pieces)
½ cup flour
¼ tsp. garlic salt
¼ tsp. onion salt

1 egg, beaten
Salt and pepper
Vegetable oil

Tenderize steak with meat mallet. Combine flour with garlic salt and onion salt. Dip each venison piece in egg, then into the seasoned flour. Sprinkle with salt and pepper to taste. Fry in hot oil until done.

Kurt Glover
Sparta, MI

Venison Fajitas

Venison Fajitas

1½ lbs. venison round steak
1 T. Adolph's meat tenderizer
½ cup lime juice
¼ cup tequila
¼ cup pickled jalapeño juice
2 T. soy sauce
1 T. chili powder
2 tsp. ground cumin
¼ cup plus 2 T. olive oil, divided
4 medium yellow onions
6 to 12 slices pickled jalapeño
1 red bell pepper
1 yellow bell pepper
1 green bell pepper
Flour tortillas, warmed just before serving
Salsa or picante sauce

Place steak in glass casserole dish. Sprinkle with meat tenderizer. In measuring cup, combine lime juice, tequila, jalapeño juice, soy sauce, chili powder and cumin; stir well. Add 2 tablespoons of the olive oil and stir again. Finely mince 1 onion and stir into to lime juice mixture. Pour over steak. Top with sliced pickled jalapeños. Cover and refrigerate overnight or up to 2 days for thicker or less tender meat.

When ready to cook, slice all the bell peppers and the remaining 3 onions into thin strips. Sauté peppers and onions in remaining ¼ cup olive oil. While vegetables are cooking, grill steak to desired doneness. Slice steak into thin strips and serve with sautéed peppers and onions, allowing each person to roll up some meat, vegetables and salsa in a flour tortilla.

Ronald Le Beaumont
and Dominique Cone
Cheyenne, WY

Shaske Venison Stew

2 to 3 lbs. venison, cut into stew cubes
¾ cup flour, seasoned with salt and pepper
1 lb. carrots, peeled and diced
1 lb. bacon
5 small or 3 large onions, thinly sliced
Butter
1 lb. mushrooms, sliced
2 (14½-oz.) cans whole or diced tomatoes
1 can corn (pick your size preference)
3 fresh tomatoes, cut into eighths

Spice mix (adjust to taste):
3 T. Tabasco sauce
2 T. Worcestershire sauce
2 T. teriyaki sauce
2 T. soy sauce
2 T. lemon juice
1 T. chili powder
2 tsp. pepper
1½ tsp. garlic powder
1½ tsp. garlic salt
1½ tsp. Lawry's seasoned salt
1½ tsp. Old Bay seasoning mix
1½ tsp. salt

Place venison in pot and add water to cover. Heat to boiling and cook until venison is brown. Drain well, discarding water. Toss venison with seasoned flour; set aside. Add carrots to pot and cover with fresh water. Heat to boiling; drain and add to slow cooker. In skillet, fry bacon until crisp. Add bacon to slow cooker, discarding grease. In same skillet, sauté onions in butter until translucent. Transfer onions to slow cooker. Sauté mushrooms in same skillet, adding additional butter if necessary. Transfer to slow cooker. Shake excess flour from meat, and add meat and remaining ingredients including spice mix to slow cooker; stir well. Add ½ cup water, or more if needed. Cook for at least 12 hours; 18 to 24 hours preferable.

Timothy L. Shaske
Bowling Green, VA

Mustard Venison

4 to 8 pieces venison cube steak
   or tenderloin
1 cup yellow mustard
1 T. plus 1½ tsp. soy sauce
½ tsp. black pepper
½ tsp. ground cayenne pepper
½ tsp. garlic salt
2 medium onions
¾ cup Coca-Cola
Vegetable oil
2 cups flour

Cut venison into 1½- to 2-inch pieces. In mixing bowl, combine mustard, soy sauce, black and cayenne pepper and salt; mix well. Slice onions ¼ inch thick and pull apart; add to mustard mixture along with venison, stirring gently to coat. Cover and refrigerate at least 2 hours; overnight is even better.

Stir Coca-Cola into meat mixture 30 minutes to 1 hour before cooking. When ready to cook, heat oil in deep fryer or deep skillet. Add flour to paper or plastic bag. Add meat and onion rings, a few pieces at a time, to bag and shake to coat. Deep-fry meat and onion rings until nicely browned.

Tommy Williams
Comer, GA

Venison Steak

1 venison steak
Flour for dusting
Olive oil
Salt and pepper
Sliced onion to taste
1 (12-oz.) can beer

Dredge steak in flour. Brown lightly in hot oil. Transfer to baking dish. Sprinkle with salt and pepper to taste; cover with sliced onion. Pour beer over all. Bake at 325°F for 1½ hours.

Steven R. Hall
Williamsport, PA

Jerked Meat Marinade

1 to 1½ lbs. brown sugar
1½ cups vinegar
1 cup liquid margarine
½ cup vegetable oil
⅓ cup salt
¼ cup black pepper
1 tsp. crumbled dried oregano leaves
1 tsp. celery salt
½ tsp. garlic powder
3 bay leaves
Dash of ground cayenne pepper

Mix ingredients in nonaluminum container and marinate any cut of venison you like for 2 to 4 days, stirring occasionally. Small strips should marinate for the shorter amount of time, while larger cuts need the longer time. This marinade is great with most any game meat, but is especially tasty for venison cooked on the grill. This makes enough marinade for up to 15 pounds of meat.

David Zembiec
Adams, NY

Deer Curry

¼ cup vegetable oil
1 large onion, sliced
6 cloves garlic, crushed
2-inch piece gingerroot, peeled and minced
1 T. curry powder
2 lbs. tenderized venison cube steak
½ tsp. salt
1 (12-oz.) can tomato sauce
½ cup water
Hot cooked rice
Pita bread or roti (Indian fried bread)

In large saucepan, heat oil over medium heat. Add onion and fry until golden brown. Add garlic and gingerroot and fry for 1 minute longer. Add curry powder and fry for 5 minutes, stirring constantly; if mixture becomes too dry, add a little water. Add venison and salt; cook for 15 minutes, or until venison is deeply browned. Add tomato sauce and water. Heat to boiling. Reduce heat and cover; simmer for 1 hour, or until venison is cooked through and tender, stirring occasionally. Serve with rice and bread.

Raymond Rivera
New York, NY

Slow-Roast Roast

3- to 4-lb. venison roast
1 (10¾-oz.) can cream of mushroom soup
1 (1½-oz.) pkg. dry onion soup mix
1 (12-oz.) can beer

Place venison in roasting pan. Cover with mushroom soup and sprinkle with onion soup. Pour beer around venison. Cover and bake at 275°F for 4 hours.

Mrs. R. Fratrick
Franklin, WI

Little Rock Style Barbecued Deer Ribs

1 side of deer ribs (3 to 4 lbs.)

LR Barbecue Rub:
¼ cup paprika
2 tsp. onion powder
2 tsp. black pepper
2 tsp. white pepper
2 tsp. salt
1 tsp. ground cayenne pepper
½ tsp. garlic powder

Shack's Barbecue Sauce:
1 (24-oz.) bottle ketchup
1½ cups white vinegar
⅓ cup sugar
3 T. prepared mustard
3 T. chili powder
2 T. garlic salt
1 T. black pepper
Hot sauce to taste

Place ribs in stockpot, cover with cold water, and simmer for 1 hour. Drain and allow to cool. Combine rub ingredients and mix well. Sprinkle on the cooled ribs, and let stand at room temperature for 1 hour while you prepare the sauce. Combine all sauce ingredients in nonaluminum saucepan and heat to a rolling boil, stirring constantly. Reduce heat and simmer for 30 minutes. When ready to cook, arrange ribs on grill, 4 to 5 inches over moderately hot coals. Cook for 15 minutes, turning once. Baste with barbecue sauce, and continue grilling until ribs are done.

Many hunters discard the ribs when dressing their deer, but savvy game chefs know this is some of the best-tasting meat on the carcass. Try them using this down-South rub and barbecue sauce, and you'll be wishing your deer were all ribs.

Keith Sutton
Alexander, AR

Venison & Sweet Potato Ragout

1 lb. tender venison, cut into bite-sized pieces
¼ cup flour, seasoned with salt and pepper
¼ cup canola oil
1 large onion, diced
2 large sweet potatoes, peeled and chunked
6 pitted prunes, halved crosswise

2 (10¾-oz.) cans beef broth
1 T. lemon juice
1 T. brown sugar
1 tsp. cracked black pepper
½ tsp. salt
1 T. cornstarch blended with ¼ cup cold water

Toss venison in seasoned flour. Heat oil in Dutch oven until hot but not smoking. Brown venison in batches, adding onions and sweet potatoes with last batch and cooking until potatoes are lightly browned. Add remaining ingredients except cornstarch/water slurry. Heat to boiling, then lower heat and simmer for 1 hour. Test venison for tenderness; if it is not tender, fish out potatoes and continue cooking venison until tender. Thicken gravy with cornstarch/water slurry; lower heat and cook for 3 minutes. Cole slaw and homemade yeast rolls go well with this dish.

Andi Flanagan
Seward, AK

Little Rock Style
Barbecued Deer Ribs

Venison Teriyaki Steak

Teriyaki marinade:
1 quart orange juice
1 quart pineapple juice
2 cups soy sauce
2 cups teriyaki sauce
 (Kikkoman's recommended)
1 lb. brown sugar
1 T. ground ginger
2 T. chopped garlic

Venison steaks
½ cup chopped fresh parsley
Sliced oranges for garnish, *optional*

Combine all marinade ingredients in heavy saucepan (preferably nonaluminum) and cook over high heat, stirring constantly, until sugar has dissolved. Reduce heat and simmer for 20 minutes. Remove from heat and let marinade cool completely; this can be made a day or two ahead and refrigerated.

Place steaks in nonmetallic container. Cover with cooled marinade and chopped parsley (reserve a little marinade for serving). Marinate venison as long as you like, turning every hour; the longer the steaks marinate the stronger the teriyaki flavor will be. Grill or broil steaks to desired doneness, turning once. Garnish steak with sliced oranges and reserved marinade.

Note: Venison grills up very well. You don't have to cook it for a long time. The tangy oriental-style teriyaki marinade adds an interesting flavor combination of ginger, orange, garlic, soy and pineapple.

Michael Gordon
Venice, FL

Canned Venison: Two Variations

Boneless venison, cut into 1- to 1½-inch
 chunks, all fat and gristle removed
Canning salt (*not* iodized table salt)
Whole garlic cloves

Follow standard canning procedures throughout. Sterilize pint or quart canning jars. Pack hot jars with venison cubes, leaving a little head space. Add 1 teaspoon canning salt to each pint jar, or 1 tablespoon canning salt to each quart jar. Add 1 or 2 cloves garlic to each jar. Seal jars tightly.

For hot-water-bath canner: Cover jars with water and heat to boiling. Boil for 3 hours for pints, 3½ hours for quarts, adding additional boiling water as necessary. Remove jars from canner and cool on rack or towel.

For pressure canner: Brown meat prior to placing in jars. Proceed as directed. Bring to 10 pounds pressure and process 70 minutes for pints, 90 minutes for quarts. Follow manufacturer's instructions for removing jars from canner.

Brent Bacon
Lewisburg, PA

No-Garlic Variation

Venison and canning salt, as above
Beef suet, cut into half-dollar-sized slices
Beef bouillon cubes

Follow instructions above, omitting garlic cloves. Add 1 piece beef suet and 1 bouillon cube to each pint jar. Seal and process as directed above (Ray recommends a water-bath canner, and boils pints for 2½ hours).

Ray McDaniel
Linden, WI

Citrus Venison & Noodles

¾ cup orange juice
3 T. soy sauce
1 T. plus 1 tsp. cornstarch
1 T. brown sugar
½ tsp. ground ginger
1 lb. boneless venison steak, cut into small strips
2 tsp. olive oil
1 (14-oz.) can diced tomatoes
2 cups frozen snow pea pods, thawed
1 pkg. (8-oz.) wide egg noodles, cooked and kept warm

In small bowl, combine orange juice, soy sauce, cornstarch, brown sugar and ginger. Mix well and set aside. In large skillet, brown venison in oil over high heat. Add orange juice mixture and tomatoes. Cook over medium heat, stirring frequently, until mixture thickens and bubbles. Add pea pods and cook for about 2 minutes longer. Serve over noodles.

Jeff Staszak and Bobbi Anne Nelson
Green Bay, WI

Spicy Fried Venison & Potatoes

2 cups canned venison cubes (1-pint jar)
1 small can whole white potatoes
¼ cup barbecue sauce
2 T. Louisiana hot sauce
3 T. vegetable oil
Garlic salt
Salt and pepper

Combine venison, potatoes, barbecue sauce and hot sauce in mixing bowl. Cover and refrigerate for 2 hours. Drain and discard excess liquid. Heat oil in large skillet; add meat and potatoes. Cook until heated and slightly crispy. Sprinkle with garlic powder, and salt and pepper to taste.

I am only 14 but I am a fine cook. I love to cook venison. This is my favorite recipe.

Alan Shetler
Bolivar, PA

Hot Roast Sandwiches

5-lb. venison roast (can also use moose, bear)
1 (10¾-oz.) can French onion soup
1 (10¾-oz.) can golden mushroom soup
1 (10¾-oz.) can cream of onion soup
1 (10¾-oz.) can cream of celery soup
½ cup water
¼ cup barbecue sauce
3 cloves garlic, chopped fine
Salt and pepper to taste
Buns or bread for serving

Place venison in roasting pan. Mix remaining ingredients except buns and pour over venison. Cover and bake at 275°F all night. In morning, shred meat with a fork and mix with sauce.

Allan H. Sly
Spooner, WI

Apple Venison Stew

2 bay leaves
2 whole allspice
2 whole cloves
2 lbs. boneless venison chuck roast,
    cut into 1½-inch cubes
2 T. butter or margarine
2 medium onions, cut into wedges
2 T. flour
1/8 tsp. salt
2 cups water
2 T. apple juice
2 medium carrots, sliced
2 medium apples, peeled and cored,
    cut into wedges
2 ribs celery, sliced
Flour or cornstarch for thickening, *optional*

Place bay leaves, allspice and cloves on a double thickness of cheesecloth. Bring up corners and tie with string to form a bag; set aside. In Dutch oven, brown venison on all sides in butter over medium heat. Add onions; cook until lightly browned. Sprinkle with flour and salt. Gradually add water and apple juice, stirring constantly. Heat to boiling; cook and stir for 2 minutes. Add spice bag. Reduce heat; cover Dutch oven and simmer for 1 to 1½ hours, or until meat is almost tender. Add carrots, apples and celery. Cover and simmer for 15 minutes longer, or until meat, carrots, apples and celery are tender. Discard spice bag. Thicken with a little flour or cornstarch mixed with a few tablespoons cold water, if desired.

James Happel
Denver, IA

Barbecued Venison

4- to 5-lb. venison roast
1 (10-oz.) can Coca-Cola
2 T. prepared mustard
2 T. liquid smoke
1 (14-oz.) bottle ketchup
¼ cup Worcestershire sauce
3 T. brown sugar

Combine all ingredients in slow cooker. Cook for 8 to 10 hours, or until tender. Shred cooked meat with fork and return to sauce.

Elbert Salsman
Amarillo, TX

Bob's Venison Roast

3 T. flour
1 large oven roasting bag
5- to 10-lb. venison shoulder, rump or
    hind quarter roast
3 or 4 cloves garlic, minced
6 to 10 whole small potatoes, peeled
3 onions, quartered
4 to 6 carrots, chunked
3 ribs celery, chopped
1 (1½-oz.) pkg. dry onion soup mix
1 (10¾-oz.) can cream of mushroom soup

Sprinkle flour into oven roasting bag; twist top and shake to distribute. Place bag in large pan. Rub top of venison roast with minced garlic, then place roast in bag. Surround roast with potatoes, onions, carrots and celery. Sprinkle onion soup mix over roast. Spread mushroom soup over roast, distributing as evenly as possible. Close and seal bag, then cut several slits in top of bag. Bake at 350°F for 2 to 3 hours, depending on size of roast.

Bob Serocke
Holland, MI

Apple Venison Stew

Rhubarb Venison

1½ lbs. venison steak, cut into bite-sized
  pieces
Vegetable oil
2 cups sliced rhubarb
½ cup sugar
2 T. flour
½ tsp. cinnamon
Hot cooked rice

In large skillet, brown venison in hot oil for 5 to 10 minutes, stirring occasionally. Drain and discard excess fat. In mixing bowl, stir together rhubarb, sugar, flour and cinnamon. Spread half of the rhubarb mixture in casserole dish. Place browned venison on top of rhubarb. Cover with remaining rhubarb mixture. Cover and bake at 350°F for 45 minutes, or until venison is tender. Serve over rice.

Russ and Marilin Branum
Greeley, CO

Pizza Steak

Venison steak
Olive oil
Italian-seasoned breadcrumbs
Whole tomatoes, crushed
Grated mozzarella or other cheese
Oregano, basil or other seasonings to taste

Dip venison in oil, then in breadcrumbs. Place on baking sheet. Cover with tomatoes, then sprinkle with cheese and herbs to taste. Bake, uncovered, at 350°F for 45 minutes to 1 hour.

Catherine Jenkins
Warren, MI

Barbecue Mex Stew

1½ lbs. lean venison stew chunks
1 cup barbecue sauce
1 cup salsa
1 (1.25-oz.) pkg. taco seasoning mix
2 cups frozen whole-kernel corn, thawed
1 (15-oz.) can chickpeas
1 (15-oz.) can black beans, rinsed and drained
½ cup chopped fresh cilantro

In slow cooker, combine all ingredients except beans and cilantro. Cover and cook on high for 4 to 5 hours, or on low for 8 to 10 hours. Stir in beans and cilantro; let stand for 5 to 10 minutes.

Jack Asher
Twin Falls, ID

Shredded Venison Roast with Lingonberries

4- to 5-lb. venison roast
3 or 4 slices bacon or fatback
1 medium yellow onion, finely chopped
1 (8-oz.) can tomato sauce
¾ cup ketchup
½ cup lingonberries or cranberries, drained
2 cloves garlic, mashed or finely chopped

3 T. Worcestershire sauce
3 T. brown sugar
2 T. cider vinegar
½ tsp. freshly ground pepper
Buns or rolls
Homemade coleslaw

Place roast in Dutch oven. Arrange bacon on top of roast. Sprinkle onion over roast and bacon. In mixing bowl, combine remaining ingredients to make thick sauce. Pour over roast. Heat over medium heat until sauce comes to rolling boil. Cover and reduce heat to low; cook for 2 hours, or until meat can be shredded with a fork (you may also bake at 325°F for 2 to 3 hours after initial boil). Remove roast from sauce and let cool for 10 to 15 minutes. Shred meat with a fork. Remove any grease from top of sauce, and return shredded meat to sauce. Serve in buns; top with coleslaw.

Michael Freitas
Cortlandt Manor, NY

Bart's Hot Texas Chili

2 lbs. venison stew meat, finely cubed
Vegetable oil
2 cups chopped onion
2 (15-oz.) cans black beans or kidney beans
1 (28-oz.) can crushed tomatoes
1 (5-oz.) can tomato sauce
1 (6-oz.) can tomato paste
4 jalapeño peppers, chopped
2 habañero peppers (Scotch bonnets), chopped
2 cloves garlic, chopped

¾ cup brown sugar
⅓ cup honey
2 T. dried parsley flakes
2 T. chili powder
2 tsp. crumbled dried oregano leaves
½ tsp. ground cumin
½ tsp. ground cayenne pepper
⅛ tsp. celery salt
⅛ tsp. black pepper
Hot cooked pasta, *optional*

In Dutch oven, brown venison in oil. Add remaining ingredients except pasta, stirring well to mix. Simmer for at least 3 hours, stirring frequently to prevent sticking. For variety, serve over pasta.

Note: This makes a very hot chili with a semi-sweet taste that keeps you going back for seconds. I sometimes use half venison and half hot sausage for variety. For a mild chili, eliminate the jalapeño peppers, habañero peppers, cumin and cayenne, and reduce chili powder to 1 tablespoon. Or, simply reduce these ingredients to adjust the heat, rather than eliminating them, to adjust the amount of heat.

Thomas "Bart" Barton
Shortsville, NY

Spicy Venison Linguini with Broccoli

Marinade:
½ cup red wine vinegar
¼ cup brown sugar
½ tsp. hot red pepper flakes
¼ tsp. ground cayenne pepper
3 cloves garlic, minced

1 lb. venison tenderloin, cut into thin strips

1 beef bouillon cube
1 cup hot water
1 lb. linguini or spaghetti
2 tsp. vegetable oil
1 bunch broccoli, separated into florets
　(4 to 5 cups florets)
2 cups low-sodium tomato sauce
15 cherry tomatoes, halved

Combine marinade ingredients in large, shallow dish. Add venison, stirring to coat; set aside. Dissolve bouillon cube in hot water; set aside. Heat a large pot of salted water to boiling. Add linguini, stirring to prevent clumping. While linguini is cooking, heat oil in large skillet over high heat until oil begins to smoke. Drain the venison, reserving marinade, and add venison to skillet, stirring frequently. Sauté until venison is nicely browned, about 3 minutes; also stir the linguini occasionally to prevent clumping.

When venison is nicely browned, use slotted spoon to transfer venison to a bowl; set aside. Reduce heat under skillet to medium, and add broccoli florets and reserved marinade. Cook until broccoli is tender, about 6 minutes. Add tomato sauce, dissolved bouillon, and browned venison to skillet.

When linguini is done, drain it well and transfer to warmed serving dish. Spoon venison, broccoli and sauce over the top, and garnish with cherry tomatoes.

Patrick Gorczyca
Jackson, MI

Dakotas Prime Rib of Venison

1 whole venison rib roast
4 cloves garlic, crushed
Salt and pepper
3 (10¾-oz.) cans beef broth

Carrots to taste, cut up
Onions to taste, cut up
Celery to taste, cut up
Potatoes to taste, cut up

Place rib roast in roasting pan. Rub roast all over with crushed garlic; salt and pepper all sides of roast generously. Add beef broth to roasting pan, and surround roast with carrots, onions, celery and potatoes. Bake at 400°F to 425°F for 1 to 1¼ hours for medium doneness; if you prefer rare, shorten baking time. Serve pan juices in a cup for dipping.

Scott Daub
Ephrata, PA

Spicy Venison Linguini with Broccoli

BIG GAME

Buffalo Rump Roast

Buffalo rump roast
Adolph's meat tenderizer (unseasoned)
⅓ cup balsamic vinegar
2 to 3 T. melted suet, or Mazola oil
1 medium to large onion, chopped
1 cup ketchup
⅓ to ½ cup cider vinegar
⅓ cup Worcestershire sauce
2 T. sugar
1 T. dry mustard
1 T. hot chili powder
1 T. ground allspice
1 tsp. black pepper

Sprinkle entire surface of roast with tenderizer; pierce meat all over with fork to allow tenderizer to penetrate. Place roast in large nonaluminum bowl, preferably with a flat bottom to fit the roast. Add balsamic vinegar and turn to coat all sides of roast. Cover bowl tightly with plastic wrap and refrigerate about 3 days, turning roast each day.

When ready to cook, pat roast dry with paper towels. Brown on all sides in suet over medium heat. Transfer browned roast to slow cooker and sprinkle with 2 to 4 tablespoons water. Soften onion in same pan used to brown roast. Add remaining ingredients and cook until sugar dissolves. Pour onion mixture over roast. Cover slow cooker and cook on high for 1 hour. Reduce heat to low and cook for 3 to 4 hours longer, or until roast is tender.

Leftover sliced roast can be rewarmed in the cooking juices the following day for sandwiches. You may also thicken the juices and add cut-up roast; serve over rice.

Bettie A. Black (Mrs. Andrew Dossett)
Albuquerque, NM

Game Cacciatore

1 lb. big-game steaks
Vegetable oil
2 onions, chopped
3 cloves garlic, minced
¼ tsp. pepper
1 (14½-oz.) can stewed tomatoes
1 (6-oz.) can tomato paste combined with
    1 cup water
½ cup red wine, *optional*
½ cup chopped fresh parsley
3 T. sugar
1 tsp. crumbled dried oregano leaves
5 cups cooked long grain wild rice

In large skillet, brown steaks in oil over medium heat. Transfer steaks to paper towel-lined plate and set aside. Add onion, garlic and pepper to drippings in skillet and sauté until onion is dark golden brown. While the onion is cooking, cut steaks into bite-sized pieces. When onion is well browned, return cut-up steaks to skillet. Add remaining ingredients except rice. Heat to boiling, then reduce heat and simmer for 15 to 20 minutes, stirring occasionally. To serve, spoon cooked rice onto individual plates and then ladle the game cacciatore onto the rice.

Denny Wood
Anchorage, AK

Best Game Sandwich

3 to 4 lbs. big-game meat
Juice from 1-quart jar of dill pickles
1 (1½-oz.) pkg. dry onion soup mix

Combine all ingredients in slow cooker; do not add water. Cook for 3 to 5 hours or until meat is done and falls off bones. Use in sandwich buns or as main table meat.

Robert Grunewald
Nekoosa, WI

Moose Steak

1 to 1½ lbs. boneless moose sirloin steak,
   about 1 inch thick
¼ cup cornstarch
1 T. dry mustard
1 tsp. salt
½ tsp. pepper
2 T. vegetable oil
1 (14½-oz.) can diced tomatoes, undrained
1 medium onion, thinly sliced
1 medium carrot, diced
Hot cooked noodles

Cut steak into serving-sized pieces. Combine cornstarch, mustard, salt and pepper. Rub half of the cornstarch mixture over one side of steak pieces. Pound with meat mallet to tenderize. Rub remaining cornstarch mixture on second side of steak pieces; pound with meat mallet. In large skillet, brown steaks on both sides in oil. Transfer browned steaks to greased 2½-quart baking dish. Top with tomatoes, onion and carrot. Cover and bake at 350°F for 1¼ to 1½ hours, or until meat is tender. Serve over noodles.

Don Wallis
Citrus Heights, CA

Caribou with Apricots

1 lb. dried apricots
4 cups water
3-lb. tender caribou roast, boned and tied
2 onions, diced
2 T. bacon drippings or vegetable oil
1 T. red wine vinegar
2 T. brown sugar
1½ tsp. salt
1 tsp. cracked black pepper
1 tsp. cinnamon
1 bay leaf

Soak apricots in water for 1 hour; do not drain. In Dutch oven, brown roast and onions in bacon drippings over medium heat. Add undrained apricots and remaining ingredients. Cover and simmer over low heat for 2½ to 3 hours, or until meat is very tender. This dish goes very well with hot cooked rice and a side dish of broccoli.

Andi Flanagan
Seward, AK

Roast Elk or Venison

Elk or venison roast
Salt and pepper
1 (8-oz.) can cranberry sauce
1 (12-oz.) bottle Russian or French dressing
1 (1½-oz.) pkg. dry onion soup mix

Place roast in roasting pan; salt and pepper to taste. In saucepan, heat cranberry sauce and dressing over low heat until cranberry sauce melts. Stir in onion soup mix. Pour cranberry mixture over roast. Bake at 275°F for approximately 4 hours, or until tender.

Bill Arrants
Brentwood, TN

Breaded Hog or Venison Backstrap Cutlets with Sautéed Mushroom Gravy

1½ lbs. feral hog or venison backstrap,
  cut ⅓ to ½ inch thick and lightly pounded
Milk
¼ cup orange juice
1 tsp. Mrs. Dash seasoning
2 tsp. salt or seasoned salt, divided
1 tsp. pepper, divided

½ cup flour
2 eggs, beaten
2 cups French bread crumbs
2 T. butter
2 T. olive oil
½ cup white wine
½ cup sliced fresh mushrooms

Place cutlets in glass bowl and cover with milk. In measuring cup, combine orange juice, Mrs. Dash seasoning, 1 teaspoon of the salt and ½ teaspoon of the pepper. Stir well, then add to bowl with cutlets and milk. Cover and refrigerate for 4 to 6 hours.

When ready to cook, place flour, eggs and bread crumbs into 3 separate shallow bowls. Stir the remaining 1 teaspoon salt and ½ teaspoon pepper into the bread crumbs. Dip cutlets one at a time, first into the flour (shaking off excess), then into the beaten eggs (allowing the excess to drip off), and then into seasoned bread crumbs. Arrange coated cutlets in a single layer on a plate or baking sheet and set aside for 15 minutes; this allows the coating to dry.

In large skillet, melt butter in oil over medium heat. Add cutlets in single layer and cook until nicely browned, 4 to 6 minutes per side. Transfer cutlets to warmed platter, retaining drippings in skillet; cover cutlets loosely and set aside. Add wine and mushrooms to skillet. Raise heat to medium-high and cook for 1 to 2 minutes, stirring frequently. Pour sauce over cutlets, or serve on the side as you prefer.

Casey C. Tate
El Paso, TX

Baked Big-Game Swiss Steak

3 lbs. cubed round steak from elk, deer, bear etc.
Flour
Cooking oil
1 (10¾-oz.) can cream of mushroom soup
1 (10½-oz.) can consommé

1 (14¾-oz.) can mushroom steak gravy
2 T. dry onion soup mix
2 tsp. prepared mustard
2 tsp. Worcestershire sauce
Hot mashed potatoes, cooked noodles or rice

Dredge steak in flour and brown in cooking oil. In blender, combine remaining ingredients and blend. Pour half the soup mixture into greased 13x9 pan, then top with browned steak. Pour remaining soup mixture over meat. Cover and bake at 350°F for 2½ hours. Serve with mashed potatoes, noodles or rice. You could also add onion, garlic or mushrooms for added flavor.

Susan Goucher (Mrs. Gilbert Goucher)
Allegan, MI

Breaded Hog Backstrap Cutlets
with Sautéed Mushroom Gravy

Moose Run Really Wild Stroganoff

1½ lbs. boneless elk, venison or bear
1 cup flour
1 tsp. pepper
1 tsp. garlic powder
½ tsp. ground cloves
Salt to taste
4 medium Vlasic country dill pickles,
  coarsely chopped (don't substitute)
1 medium red onion, halved and thinly sliced

8 large button mushrooms, thinly sliced
6 cloves elephant garlic, sliced or chopped
4 to 6 T. butter (half to three-quarters
  of a stick)
¾ cup cabernet sauvignon
¾ cup beef broth
⅔ cup sour cream
Hot cooked egg noodles
Hungarian paprika for garnish

Trim elk of all fat and cut into ½-inch chunks. Combine flour, pepper, garlic powder, cloves and salt to taste. Dredge elk cubes in seasoned flour and set aside. In large skillet or Dutch oven, cook pickles, onion, mushrooms and garlic in butter over high heat for 5 minutes, stirring constantly. Add floured elk and cook for 10 minutes longer. Add wine, broth and sour cream, stirring well. Lower heat, cover and simmer for about 25 minutes, or until meat is tender, stirring occasionally; add a little additional broth if the mixture seems to be drying out. Serve over egg noodles and sprinkle with paprika.

Robert W. Dixon
Sandpoint, ID

Sourdough Elk or Venison Steak

3 lbs. elk or venison steak
1 cup flour
2 tsp. onion salt
2 tsp. paprika

2 tsp. pepper
1 cup sourdough starter (recipe below)
¾ cup vegetable oil, shortening or lard

Pound steak to ½-inch thickness with meat mallet or heavy knife. Cut into serving pieces. Combine flour, onion salt, paprika and pepper. Dip steaks in sourdough starter, then into flour mixture. Heat 1 inch oil in heavy skillet, and fry steaks until done.

Sourdough Starter

1 quart lukewarm water
1 (¼-oz.) pkg. dry yeast

2 tsp. sugar
4 cups flour

Put water in crock or large glass jar. Add yeast and sugar to soften, then stir in flour. Cover with clean cloth. Let rise until mixture is light and slightly aged, about 2 days. Mixture will be thin as it stands; add flour as needed. As you use sourdough from the crock, replace it with equal amounts of flour and water.

Sonny (Grizz) and Terri Adams
Kremmling, CO

Shredded Carne

1 wild hog or venison shoulder
1 large onion, coarsely chopped
1 bell pepper, coarsely chopped
5 cloves garlic, chopped
1 fresh jalapeño pepper, *optional*
2 T. Worcestershire sauce
Salt and pepper to taste

Grill or smoke hog shoulder until rare. Place meat in large pot and cover with water. Add remaining ingredients. Simmer over low heat until meat falls off the bone, being careful not to boil. Remove and discard bones. Shred meat and return to the pot. Continue to cook over low heat until most of the water is gone; if meat is very lean a little oil can be added.

This recipe produces quite a bit of meat that can be used in tacos, sandwiches etc. It can be frozen for later use or to be taken on a future hunting trip. I have found this method to be easier and less wasteful than seaming out the shoulder meat.

Casey C. Tate
El Paso, TX

Bear Pot Roast

Marinade:
½ cup vegetable oil
¼ cup lemon juice
2 cloves garlic, crushed
1 bay leaf
1 tsp. crumbled dried thyme leaves
1 tsp. salt
½ tsp. pepper

4- to 5-lb. bear rump roast
4 large potatoes, quartered
10 whole baby carrots
8 small boiling onions, peeled

Combine all marinade ingredients in large leakproof plastic bag; place bag in large dish for support. Remove fat and bone from roast; tie securely. Place roast in bag with marinade, force all air out top of bag and seal securely. Marinate in refrigerator for 6 to 8 hours, or as long as overnight.

When ready to cook, place roast and marinade in roasting pan. Cover and bake at 350°F for 30 minutes per pound. Add potatoes, baby carrots and boiling onions to pan with roast during last hour of cooking. Make gravy from pan juices if desired. To serve, place roast on large serving platter and arrange vegetables around roast. Serve gravy on the side.

Defort Bailey
Irvine, KY

Smoky Bear Bobs

Smoky Bear-Bobs

Marinade:
1 cup soy sauce
1/3 cup sherry
2 T. brown sugar
1 T. ketchup
1 T. molasses
1 T. minced onion
1 tsp. liquid smoke
1 tsp. grated fresh gingerroot
2 cloves garlic, minced

3 lbs. boneless bear, cut into chunks
Cherry tomatoes
Green bell pepper chunks
Small puffballs or button mushrooms
Pineapple chunks
Hot cooked rice

Combine all marinade ingredients in nonaluminum bowl. Add bear, stirring to coat. Cover and refrigerate overnight.

When ready to cook, preheat grill or broiler. Thread meat, vegetables and pineapple chunks alternately on skewers and grill until bear is well-done; for safety it should read 185°F on a meat thermometer. Heat remaining marinade to boiling, and serve with rice and bear-bobs.

Cold beer and cole slaw go well with this. Have something blueberry for dessert and honor the bear.

Andi Flanagan
Seward, AK

Game Roast in Foil

4- to 6-lb. moose, elk or venison roast
1/2 lb. sliced bacon
3 or 4 slices lemon
1/2 cup red wine
1 (1½-oz.) pkg. dry onion soup mix
Salt and pepper to taste

Place roast in center of a double layer of foil. Add remaining ingredients. Seal package and place in roasting pan. Bake at 350°F for 2½ to 3 hours. Slice meat and serve with juices, or thicken juices to make gravy and serve with wild rice.

William P. Crewe
Seaford, DE

Moose Round Steak

2 lbs. moose round steak
1 T. bacon drippings
1½ cups red wine
1/2 cup beef broth
1 tsp. salt
1/2 tsp. crumbled dried thyme leaves
2 cloves garlic, chopped
1 onion, chopped
Half an orange, cut into small strips
2 T. cornstarch blended with 2 T. cold water
1 cup fresh mushrooms, sliced
1 (16-oz.) can small onions, drained
1/2 cup pitted black olives
1 (10-oz.) pkg. frozen peas

In large skillet, brown steak in bacon drippings. Add wine, broth, salt, thyme, garlic, onion and orange strips. Cover and simmer for 1½ hours or until tender. Add cornstarch/water slurry and cook until liquid is thickened. Add remaining ingredients; cook until heated through. Remove orange slices before serving.

Lloyd L. Prochnow
Elk Mound, WI

Slow-Cooked Peppered Elk

2-lb. elk roast
Flour
Olive oil
2 T. Mrs. Dash seasoning
1 tsp. salt
½ tsp. black pepper
2 medium onions, sliced
20 pepperoncini peppers
1 cup juice from pepperoncini peppers
6 cloves garlic, cut into quarters

Dredge roast in flour. In Dutch oven or deep frying pan, brown roast on all sides in olive oil over medium heat. Season roast with Mrs. Dash, salt and black pepper. Add remaining ingredients. Cover and cook on low heat until meat is fork tender; cooking time will range from 2 to 4 hours depending on thickness of the roast. A small amount of liquid should be present during cooking at all times; if the liquid runs low, add a little water. Serve with crusty French bread. This dish could also be prepared in a slow cooker or pressure cooking, following the instructions for the appliance.

Before hunting trips, we prepare the Slow Cooked Peppered Elk, then package it in vacuum bags and freeze it. At camp, once it's thawed, we pour the contents of the bag into a frying pan to heat it, and serve with bread or rolls. This was a big hit from the start, and now has become a tradition.

Al and Kathy Kelley
Yuma, AZ

Wapiti Tin Plate Special

1 lb. dry pinto beans
6-lb. elk roast
1 T. lard, shortening or bacon drippings
1 cup sweet banana pepper or green bell pepper strips
2 medium onions, peeled and sliced
2 cups tomato juice
1 (8-oz.) can tomato paste
½ cup water
2 T. cider vinegar
2 T. brown sugar
2 tsp. salt
1 tsp. dry mustard
1 tsp. crumbled dried thyme leaves

Wash and sort beans; cover with cold water and let soak overnight. Heat beans to boiling and cook for 1 hour; drain, discarding cooking water. In Dutch oven or roaster, brown roast in lard. Add peppers and onions and cook until vegetables are tender. Add beans and remaining ingredients to Dutch oven. Cover and bake at 350°F for 2½ to 3 hours, or until beans are tender and meat is done.

This recipe can be used for all wild game meat, or even domestic meat.

Sonny and Terri Adams
Kremmling, CO

Antelope Parmesan

8 boneless antelope loin chops, 1 inch thick
1 T. Adolph's meat tenderizer
1½ cups milk, divided
2 eggs
½ cup Italian-seasoned breadcrumbs
¼ cup olive oil
1 tsp. garlic powder or granulated garlic
1 tsp. crumbled dried oregano leaves
1 tsp. crumbled dried basil leaves
⅛ tsp. hot red pepper flakes, *optional*
1 (28-oz.) can crushed tomatoes
½ cup shredded mozzarella cheese
Hot cooked pasta

Place antelope chops in small casserole dish. Sprinkle chops with tenderizer. Cover with about ¾ cup of the milk, agitating gently to mix the tenderizer into the milk. Cover and refrigerate overnight.

When ready to cook, discard milk and rinse chops in cold water. Pound chops with meat mallet until ¼ to ½ inch thick. Beat eggs with the remaining ¾ cup milk. Dip chops in egg mixture, then dredge in breadcrumbs. Sauté in olive oil until golden brown. Place browned chops in large pyrex casserole pan. Add garlic powder, oregano, basil and red pepper to tomatoes and pour over chops, covering them well. Sprinkle with mozzarella cheese. Cover casserole and bake at 350°F for 30 minutes. Uncover casserole and bake for 5 minutes longer, or until cheese is slightly browned and bubbly. Serve with your favorite cooked pasta and red wine.

Ronald Le Beaumont
and Dominique Cone
Cheyenne, WY

Heart Stew

1 big game heart
1 large potato, diced
½ cup sliced celery
½ cup sliced carrot
¼ cup diced onion
1 T. beef base
½ tsp. garlic powder
¼ tsp. pepper
1 quart water

Boil heart until well done. Wash in cold water. Dice into ½-inch cubes; set aside. Combine remaining ingredients in medium pot and cook until vegetables are tender but still firm. Add diced heart to pot. Reduce heat and simmer for 30 to 45 minutes.

David Pehler
Winona, MN

Wild Hog Chili

2 lbs. lean hog meat, cut into ½-inch cubes
Half of an onion, diced
3 or 4 fresh hot peppers, diced
2 T. vegetable oil
2 (15-oz.) cans pinto beans with bacon
2 (15-oz.) cans crushed tomatoes
2 T. chili powder
2 tsp. salt
1 tsp. ground cumin

In large pot, brown hog, onion and peppers in oil; do not drain. Add remaining ingredients (do not drain canned items) and heat to boiling. Reduce heat; cover and simmer for 2 to 3 hours, stirring occasionally, until meat is very tender.

Mike Read
Pearland, TX

Savory Pepper Elk Steak

¼ cup flour
½ tsp. salt
¼ tsp. pepper
1½ lbs. elk round steak, cut into strips
¼ cup shortening
1 (14-oz.) can Mexican-style stewed tomatoes
   with jalapeño peppers
1½ cups warm water
½ cup chopped onion

1 clove garlic, minced
1 T. beef-flavored gravy base
¼ cup sherry
1½ tsp. Worcestershire sauce
1 large green bell pepper, cut into strips
1 to 2 T. flour blended with an equal amount
   cold water, *optional*
Hot cooked rice

Combine flour, salt and pepper. Dredge steak strips in seasoned flour. Heat shortening in large skillet or Dutch oven, and brown steak strips over medium heat. Drain the tomatoes, reserving liquid. Add tomato liquid, water, onion, garlic and gravy base to skillet. Reduce heat; cover and simmer for 1½ hours or until meat is tender. Add sherry, Worcestershire sauce and bell pepper strips to skillet. Re-cover and simmer for 5 minutes. (If gravy is too thin, thicken with the optional flour/water slurry. Stir into sauce, and cook until thick and bubbly.) Add drained tomatoes and cook for 5 minutes longer. Serve over rice.

This is one of the ways we like elk cooked in the high country in Arizona (elevation 7,000 feet). All my friends and relatives rave about this dish. My brothers in the Hunting Club will, too.

Jesse E. Taylor
Happy Jack, AZ

French Onion Elk Au Jus

2 large onions, sliced
4 T. butter (half of a stick)
3- to 4-lb. elk roast (can also use venison)
1¼ quarts water
½ cup soy sauce
1 (1½-oz.) pkg. dry onion soup mix

1½ tsp. browning sauce such as
   Kitchen Bouquet
⅛ tsp. garlic powder
Hoagie buns
1 cup shredded Swiss or mozzarella cheese

Sauté onion in butter until tender. Add to Dutch oven with remaining ingredients except buns and cheese. Cover and bake at 325°F for 2 hours, or until roast is tender. Remove roast and let stand for 20 minutes before slicing. Slice thinly across the grain and return to cooking liquid. Toast the buns under the broiler. Place sliced roast on buns, top with cheese, and return to oven until cheese melts. Serve with meat juices poured over the sandwiches; or, serve the juices in a small bowl for dipping.

This recipe works great in a slow cooker, too; cook for 8 to 10 hours on low heat.

Jason Vander Werff
Pella, IA

Savory Pepper Elk Steak

Bear Stew

2 lbs. boneless bear meat, cut into stew cubes
1 tsp. salt
Dash pepper
Vegetable oil
2 cups water
3 beef bouillon cubes
3 carrots, sliced
2 potatoes, cubed
2 onions, cut into quarters
½ cup thinly sliced celery
3 T. Worcestershire sauce
Flour blended with water for thickening

Sprinkle bear cubes with salt and pepper. In Dutch oven, brown bear cubes in vegetable oil over medium heat. Add water and bouillon cubes. Cover; reduce heat and simmer for about 1 hour, or until meat is becoming tender, stirring occasionally. Add remaining ingredients except flour slurry. Re-cover and simmer for 1 hour longer, stirring occasionally. Thicken gravy with flour slurry.

Ronald Bergman
Tripoli, WI

Delicious Grilled Bison

Bison steak
Italian dressing

Marinate steak in dressing for 3 or 4 days. Remove from marinade. Grill over low heat for 3 to 4 minutes each side (rare). Bison is a lean meat, so remember when cooking: lower and slower.

Sally Shaffer
Dixon, SD

Elk Rouladen

8 slices elk steak (about 2 lbs.)
Dijon mustard
Salt and pepper
8 slices bacon
1 large onion, cut into thin wedges
3 T. vegetable oil
3 cups beef broth
⅓ cup flour
½ cup water

Pound steak slices to ¼-inch thickness. Lightly spread mustard on each slice; sprinkle with salt and pepper. Place 1 slice bacon and a few onion wedges on each steak slice; roll up and secure with wooden toothpicks. In large skillet, brown rolls in vegetable oil; drain and discard excess oil. Add broth to skillet and heat to boiling. Reduce heat; cover and simmer for 1½ hours or until meat is tender. Remove meat from skillet and keep warm. In small bowl, combine flour and water, stirring until smooth. Stir flour slurry into broth in skillet. Heat to boiling, stirring constantly, and cook until sauce thickens and bubbles. Remove toothpicks from elk rolls and return rolls to gravy. Cook until meat is heated through.

Robert Gailey
Nezperce, ID

Bear's Mango Elk

½ cup red wine
½ tsp. cornstarch
1 lb. boneless elk, cut into 1-inch cubes
1 mango
1 bell pepper, cored and seeded
1 (8-oz.) can pineapple rings, drained
2 tsp. olive oil
½ tsp. minced fresh gingerroot
1 apple, peeled, cored and cut into
   1-inch cubes
2 tsp. plum sauce, *optional*
Hot cooked rice

In mixing bowl, combine wine and cornstarch, stirring well. Add elk, stirring to coat; cover and refrigerate overnight.

When ready to cook, peel mango and cut flesh away from pit; cut mango into 1-inch cubes. Slice bell pepper into ½-inch strips, then cut strips at a 45-degree angle to make diamonds. Cut pineapple rings into quarters.

Heat wok or large skillet over high heat. Add oil and ginger to hot wok; cook and stir until ginger is lightly browned. Add elk and half of the wine marinade; cook and stir until meat starts to glaze. Add mango, bell pepper and apple. Reduce heat to medium. Cook and stir until apple starts to brown, about 2 minutes. Add pineapple and plum sauce. Continue cooking and stirring until pineapple is heated through. Serve over rice.

John "Bear" Black
Hayward, CA

Moose Rump Roast

6-lb. moose rump roast
6 (12-oz.) bottles dark ale beer
4 baking potatoes, cut into 1-inch cubes
3 large carrots, peeled and cut into 2-inch logs
2 parsnips, cut into 1-inch cubes
1 large onion, cut into large chunks
2 cloves garlic, finely chopped
1 T. curry powder
1 tsp. Indian ginger
1 tsp. ground coriander
Salt and pepper

Poke roast all over with fork. Truss meat into loaf shape and tie with string. Place in large bowl. Pour ale over roast; cover and refrigerate overnight.

Remove roast from marinade and place in large roasting pan, discarding marinade. Surround roast with potatoes, carrots, parsnips, onion and garlic. Cover roaster with foil. Bake at 350°F for about 3 hours (4 hours if you are at 5000 feet or higher in elevation).

While meat is roasting, combine curry powder, ginger and coriander in small bowl. When roast has cooked the amount of time noted above, sprinkle spice mixture over roast. Return to oven and cook for 1 hour longer. To serve, remove string and slice roast into ½-inch-thick slices. Serve with vegetables; salt and pepper to taste.

In 1968, Papa and I got tags for hunting moose in British Columbia. After establishing camp, we went hunting. By about 1:00 p.m., Papa brought down a trophy 12-point bull moose. After field dressing, Papa cut out a big chunk of moose rump and told me to prepare a proper roast for supper the next day. I prepared the meat in the old-world way as written above. That next morning, I took down my first 3-point bull moose. What a thrill for this (then) 18-year-old woman!

Kaylan Ardora
Tacoma, WA

GROUND VENISON & OTHER GAME

Venison Logs

1 cup tomato juice
2 eggs, beaten
4 cups bread stuffing cubes
2 tsp. seasoned salt
1 tsp. celery salt
1 tsp. liquid smoke
2 lbs. ground venison
16 slices American cheese
16 frankfurter rolls, lightly buttered

In large mixing bowl, combine tomato juice, eggs, bread cubes, seasoned salt, celery salt and liquid smoke; mix very well. Add ground venison and mix well. Cover and refrigerate for 30 minutes. Divide mixture into 16 portions. Form each portion into a log shape about 4 inches long. Grill logs over hot coals until done. Place 1 slice American cheese onto each frankfurter roll; place cooked log on top of cheese.

David Miller
Harriman, NY

Venison Pasta Sauce

2 lbs. ground venison
½ lb. ground dove or other game bird
2 medium onions, chopped
4 (8-oz.) cans stewed tomatoes
1 (6-oz.) can tomato paste
¼ cup chopped fresh parsley
2 T. Italian seasoning blend
Salt to taste

In large saucepan, brown venison and dove; add onions near end of browning. When onions are tender, add remaining ingredients. Heat to gentle boil and stir. Reduce heat and simmer for up to 5 hours, stirring frequently.

Richard Martino
Woodland, CA

Tater Tot Casserole

1½ lbs. ground venison, elk or moose
1 tsp. salt
¼ tsp. pepper
¼ cup chopped onion
1 (8-oz.) can French-style green beans, drained
1 (8-oz.) can whole-kernel corn, drained
1 (10¾-oz.) can cheddar cheese soup
1 (1-lb.) pkg. tater tots

Season venison with salt and pepper. Brown with onion. Pat into bottom of 13×9×2-inch dish. Top evenly with beans and corn. Spread soup evenly over vegetables; top evenly with tater tots. Bake at 350°F until hot.

Carl Bartelt
Hillsboro, WI

Picadillo

2 lbs. ground venison
2 (15-oz.) cans beef consommé
2 (15-oz.) cans diced tomatoes
2 (6-oz.) cans tomato paste
2 bottles cocktail onions, drained
2 (3-oz.) pkgs. slivered almonds
1 (6-oz.) can black olives, chopped
1 (6-oz.) can mushroom pieces and stems, drained
6 green onions, finely chopped

4 potatoes, diced
1 green bell pepper, chopped
2 cloves garlic, chopped
2 jalapeño peppers, seeded and chopped
1 cup diced pimientos
1 cup raisins
Seasonings to taste: Salt, ground cayenne pepper, paprika, ground cumin, oregano and Worcestershire sauce

In large skillet, brown venison over medium heat, stirring to break up. Add remaining ingredients except seasoning; stir well to mix. Season to taste as you like it. Simmer mixture over medium heat until potatoes are tender, about 20 minutes, stirring occasionally. Serve as a hot dip with chips.

Joe and Becky Stahl
Fort Richardson, AK

Venison, Elk or Antelope Tamale Pie

1 lb. ground venison, elk or antelope
1 (8-oz.) can whole tomatoes
1 (8-oz.) can whole-kernel corn
1 cup cornmeal
3 eggs
2 cups milk

½ cup vegetable oil
1 large onion, chopped
½ tsp. black pepper
1 tsp. ground cayenne pepper
Pitted ripe olives

In large skillet, cook venison over medium heat until cooked through, stirring to break up; set aside. In saucepan, cook tomatoes and corn until juices cook away, about 15 minutes. In large mixing bowl, combine cornmeal, eggs and milk. Stir until thick. Add cooked venison, tomato mixture, oil, onion, black pepper and cayenne pepper and mix very well. Pour into greased 13×9×2-inch baking dish. Garnish with olives. Bake at 350°F for 50 to 60 minutes.

Arthur Van Dommelen
De Pere, WI

Queso Subs

Queso Subs

1 lb. ground venison
1 T. vegetable oil
1 onion, diced
1 green bell pepper, diced
1 (28-oz.) can whole tomatoes, undrained
2 tsp. green jalapeño Tabasco sauce
1 tsp. chili powder
1/4 tsp. ground cumin
8 hard rolls
2 cups medium cheddar cheese, grated

In large skillet, brown venison in oil over medium heat. Push meat to one side, then add onion and bell pepper and sauté until vegetables are soft. Add tomatoes including juice, Tabasco sauce, chili powder and cumin and mix well. Let mixture simmer until excess liquid has been absorbed but sauce is still moist, about 20 minutes. While mixture cooks, slice off the tops of the rolls and pull out most of the doughy insides. Place hollowed-out rolls on cookie sheet and warm them in a 300°F oven for about 10 minutes, so rolls are ready about the same time as the sauce. To serve, spoon 3 or 4 tablespoons of meat sauce into each roll, top with cheddar cheese and return to oven until cheese melts, about 5 minutes. Serve with warm tortilla chips and lots of napkins.

Frank Bruno
Dubois, WY

Lloyd's Venison Loaf

1 1/2 cups chopped onion
2 T. butter
1 1/2 cups shredded carrot
1 1/2 cups shredded potato
2 lbs. ground venison
1 large tomato, peeled and chopped;
    or 1 (16-oz.) can diced tomato
2 eggs
1 cup breadcrumbs
1/2 tsp. nutmeg
1/2 tsp. garlic powder
Salt and pepper to taste

In large skillet, sauté onion in butter until just tender. Add carrot and potato. Cover and cook 5 minutes longer. Transfer to large mixing bowl. Add remaining ingredients and mix well. Shape into loaf in greased shallow baking dish. Bake at 350°F for 1 hour.

Lloyd Prochnow
Elk Mound, WI

Deer Stand Salad

2 cups browned venison burger
1/2 cup salad dressing (your choice)
1/2 cup chopped sweet pickles
1/4 cup chopped onion
2 hard-cooked eggs, chopped

Mix all ingredients. Serve as a sandwich filling or as a salad. Great on toast.

Harold "Scottie" Scott
Cincinnati, OH

Venison Pâté

½ lb. ground venison
½ lb. pork sausage
1 cup finely shredded carrot
½ cup fine, dry breadcrumbs
½ cup chopped pecans
½ cup chopped onion
¼ cup C.C. Cask sherry, *optional*
1 egg, beaten
¼ tsp. salt
¼ tsp. crumbled dried oregano leaves
¼ tsp. pepper

Combine all ingredients in large bowl; mix well. Pack lightly into 7½×3½-inch loaf pan. Bake at 350°F for 1 hour, or until well done. Drain and discard excess juices; cool pâté. Refrigerate until completely cold. Slice and serve as an appetizer.

Kenneth W. Crummett
Sugar Grove, WV

Moose Pizza

1 lb. ground moose
⅔ cup evaporated milk
½ cup fine, dry breadcrumbs
1 tsp. garlic salt
⅓ cup ketchup
¼ cup sliced mushrooms
1 cup shredded cheddar cheese
2 T. grated Parmesan cheese
¼ tsp. crumbled dried oregano leaves

Mix together moose, milk, breadcrumbs and garlic salt. Pat evenly into 9-inch pie plate. Spread ketchup over meat. Top with mushrooms and cheddar cheese. Sprinkle with Parmesan cheese and oregano. Bake at 350°F for 25 minutes.

Glenn Clark

Porcupine Balls

½ lb. ground venison
½ lb. ground beef
1½ cups uncooked instant rice, such as Minute Rice
½ tsp. garlic powder, or to taste
Dash of salt
1 (10¾-oz.) can condensed tomato soup
Hot cooked rice or mashed potatoes

In mixing bowl, combine venison, beef, instant rice, garlic powder and salt. Mix well, and form into golfball-sized balls. Place meatballs in roasting pan. Cover meatballs with tomato soup; rinse soup can with a little water and add to roasting pan. Cover roasting pan and bake at 350°F for 2 hours. Serve with rice or mashed potatoes.

George Sanders
Sudbury, ONT

Cowboy Casserole

1 lb. ground venison
1 medium onion, chopped
1 (10-oz.) pkg. bacon, cut into pieces
1 (15-oz.) can pork and beans
1 (15-oz.) can kidney beans, drained
1 (15-oz.) can butter beans, drained
1 (15-oz.) can navy beans, drained
¾ cup brown sugar
½ cup ketchup
2 T. vinegar
2 T. prepared mustard

In skillet, brown venison and onion, stirring to break up meat; drain. Fry bacon until crisp; drain. Combine all ingredients in slow cooker and mix well; cover and cook for 2 to 3 hours. Or, place in casserole and bake at 350°F for 1 to 1½ hours.

Randy and Sharon Russell
Burlington, IA

Venison Egg Rolls

1 lb. ground venison
1½ cups shredded cabbage
1 (8-oz.) can cream of mushroom soup
1 (4-oz.) can sliced mushrooms, drained
1 (2-oz.) can sliced black olives
1 (1½-oz.) pkg. dry onion soup mix
Jalapeño peppers to taste, chopped
1 (16-oz.) pkg. egg roll wraps
Vegetable oil
Sour cream for garnish
Shredded cheddar cheese for garnish

In skillet, cook venison until about half-done, stirring to break up. Add cabbage and cook for 2 to 3 minutes longer. Add mushroom soup, sliced mushrooms, olives, dry soup mix and jalapeño peppers; mix well. Place 1 tablespoon meat mixture on egg roll wrap. Roll up and seal as directed on egg-roll package. Deep fry at 350°F until golden brown. Garnish with sour cream and cheddar cheese.

Terry Gilbert
Alexander, AR

Deer Burger Casserole

1 lb. ground venison
1 medium onion, chopped
2 boxes refrigerated pie crust
1 (32-oz.) jar peppers and sauce
1 (12-oz.) pkg. shredded Co-Jack cheese

In skillet, cook venison and onion until venison is no longer pink, stirring to break up meat. Line bottom and sides of 13×9×2-inch baking dish with 2 pie crusts. Spread half of the peppers and sauce over the crust. Top with meat mixture; cover with remaining peppers and sauce. Sprinkle Co-Jack cheese evenly over all. Top with 1½ of the remaining pie crusts. Bake at 350°F for 40 to 45 minutes, or until crust is golden.

Richie Taylor
Bridgeport, WV

BC's Sheep Chili

1½ lbs. ground sheep
3 cups chili beans
1 (14½-oz.) can chopped tomatoes, undrained
1½ (14½-oz.) cans tomato sauce
½ cup chopped black olives
1 cup water
1 tsp. salt
1 tsp. black pepper
1 tsp. red pepper
Chili powder to taste
Chopped onion for garnish
Shredded pepper-Jack cheese for garnish

In Dutch oven, brown sheep over medium heat, stirring to break up. Drain and discard excess grease. Add all remaining ingredients except onion and cheese. Simmer for about 4 hours. Serve with chopped onion and grated cheese. Good with corn bread.

Brian Cape
Palmer, AK

Venison Meatballs with Sauerkraut & Cranberry Sauce

2 lbs. ground venison
1 cup cracker crumbs
3 eggs, beaten
½ of (1½-oz.) pkg. dry onion soup mix

1 (12-oz.) can whole-berry cranberry sauce
1 cup sauerkraut, rinsed and drained
1 cup brown sugar
¼ cup barbecue sauce

In large mixing bowl, combine venison, cracker crumbs, eggs and onion soup mix. Form into meatballs. Place in 13×9×2-inch baking dish. Mix remaining ingredients in separate bowl. Spread cranberry mixture evenly over meatballs. Bake uncovered at 325°F for 1 hour.

This is a very unusual dish, but top notch! These sweet and tangy venison meatballs are perfect for the holiday season or any time. They can be served as an appetizer or a main dish.

Mike Collins
Howell, MI

Venison Stuffed Mushrooms

1 lb. ground venison
¼ lb. Jimmy Dean spiced pork sausage
1 cup chopped onion
1 lb. large mushrooms such as portobello
¾ cup water
1 T. finely chopped fresh parsley
½ tsp. salt

⅛ tsp. pepper
½ cup uncooked instant rice, such as
    Minute Rice
¾ cup mayonnaise
½ cup grated Parmesan cheese
½ cup Italian-seasoned breadcrumbs
Louisiana hot sauce to taste

In medium skillet, begin cooking venison and sausage, stirring to break up; add onions when meat starts to brown. Meanwhile, remove stems from mushrooms. Chop stems finely and add to meat mixture; cook until lightly browned. Add water, parsley, salt and pepper. Heat to boiling. Stir in instant rice. Cover and remove from heat; let stand for 5 minutes.

In small bowl, mix mayonnaise and Parmesan cheese. Stir ½ cup of the mayonnaise mixture into the meat mixture. Add breadcrumbs and mix well. Spoon meat mixture into mushroom caps. Place filled mushroom caps in shallow baking dish. Top with remaining mayonnaise mixture. Bake at 400°F for about 15 minutes, or until golden brown and puffy. Serve with hot sauce.

Mike Westrick
St. Clair, MI

Mexican Venison Casserole (*page 58*)

Venison Meatballs with Sauerkraut & Cranberry Sauce

Venison Stuffed Mushrooms

Mexican Venison Casserole *(pictured on page 57)*

1 lb. ground venison
1 lb. ground sausage
1 cup cooked white rice
1 (24-oz.) jar salsa
1 (16-oz.) can refried beans
1 (12-oz.) pkg. shredded cheddar cheese
Soft flour tortillas, or tortilla chips

Garnishes of your choice:
Shredded lettuce
Sour cream
Chopped green onions
Chopped green chilies
Chopped tomatoes

In large skillet, brown venison and sausage, stirring to break up. Drain and discard excess grease. Add cooked rice and salsa, stirring to combine. Set aside. Warm refried beans slightly in microwave or on stovetop, then spread over the bottom of a 13×9×2-inch baking dish. Top beans with meat mixture; sprinkle cheddar cheese evenly over meat. Bake at 350°F for 25 to 30 minutes. Garnish with any or all of the garnishes and serve with warm flour tortillas. This also makes a great dip for tortilla chips.

Don Woodcock
Alma, MI

Crock Pot Venison Cabbage Casserole

1 lb. ground venison
1 large onion, chopped
½ cup cooked rice
1 (10¾-oz.) can condensed tomato soup
¼ cup water
Seasoned salt and pepper
4 cups shredded cabbage
Sour cream, *optional*
Diced green onions, *optional*

In medium skillet, cook venison and onion until venison is browned, stirring to break up meat. Drain and discard excess grease. Stir in cooked rice, tomato soup, water, and salt and pepper to taste. Place cabbage in slow cooker; spoon meat mixture over cabbage. Cover and cook on low for 4 to 5 hours; do not stir during cooking. Garnish with sour cream and diced green onions.

Jim Kilgore
Bellevue, KY

Elk Burgers

2 lbs. ground elk
¾ cup chili sauce
¼ cup Worcestershire sauce
¼ cup fine breadcrumbs
2 cloves garlic, minced
2 T. brandy, *optional*
1 egg, beaten
Salt and pepper to taste
6 slices bacon, cut into halves

In large mixing bowl, combine all ingredients except bacon. Mix well and form into 6 patties. Top burgers with bacon strips while cooking. Cook until inside temperature is 145°F.

Jack Clark
Superior, WI

Venison Spanish Delight

1 medium onion, chopped
1 medium bell pepper, chopped
2 T. margarine
1 lb. ground venison
½ tsp. salt
2 garlic cloves, minced
2 cups uncooked noodles
4 cups salted water
1 (14½-oz.) can sliced mushrooms, drained
1 (14½-oz.) can tomato sauce with cheese
1 (3.8-oz.) can ripe olives, drained
1 (15¼-oz.) can whole-kernel corn
2 T. chili powder
1 cup shredded cheddar cheese

In large skillet, sauté onion and bell pepper in margarine until just tender. Add venison and salt and continue cooking until venison is browned, stirring to break up meat. When venison is browned, stir garlic into skillet. Remove from heat; set aside.

Cook noodles until tender in boiling salted water; drain well. Combine meat mixture, cooked noodles, and all remaining ingredients except shredded cheese. Pour into pyrex baking dish or casserole. Top with shredded cheddar cheese. Bake at 350°F for 45 minutes, Serve with a salad of your choice.

Mary Greider
Houston, TX

Venison with Wild Rice

1 lb. ground venison
1½ cups cooked wild rice
1 (10¾-oz.) can cream of chicken soup
1 (10¾-oz.) can cream of mushroom soup
1 medium onion, chopped
1 cup sliced celery
1 cup sliced mushrooms
1 cup water
3 T. soy sauce

In large skillet, brown venison over medium heat, stirring to break up. Add remaining ingredients and mix well. Pour into 2-quart casserole dish. Cover and bake at 350°F for 30 minutes. Uncover and bake for 30 minutes longer.

Tommy Williams
Comer, GA

Venison Lasagna

Venison Lasagna

2 lbs. ground venison
Bacon drippings
1 clove garlic, minced
1 tsp. dried parsley flakes
1 tsp. dried basil leaves
1 (16-oz.) can tomatoes, undrained
2 (6-oz.) cans tomato paste
½ of (16-oz.) pkg. lasagna noodles
2 eggs, beaten
2 (12-oz.) cartons cream-style cottage cheese
    or ricotta cheese
½ cup grated Parmesan cheese
½ tsp. pepper
1 lb. mozzarella cheese, sliced

In large skillet, brown venison in bacon drippings, stirring to break up. Drain and discard excess grease. Add garlic, parsley flakes, basil, tomatoes with their juices, and tomato paste. Simmer about 15 minutes or until thick, stirring occasionally. Meanwhile, cook lasagna noodles according to package directions; drain. In mixing bowl, combine eggs, cottage cheese, Parmesan cheese and pepper; mix well.

Spread about ½ cup meat sauce in greased 13×9×2-inch baking dish. Top with half of the cooked lasagna noodles. Spread half the cottage cheese mixture over the noodles. Arrange half the sliced mozzarella cheese over the cottage cheese, and top with half the remaining meat sauce. Repeat layers. Cover and bake at 350°F for 45 minutes; let stand 10 minutes before cutting into serving pieces.

Wayne Marksbury
Lexington Park, MD

Elk Chili

2 lbs. ground elk
¼ cup vegetable oil
1 large onion, chopped
1 green bell pepper, chopped
3 ribs celery, sliced
1 cup sliced fresh mushrooms
6 ripe medium tomatoes, peeled
    and quartered
1 medium zucchini, cut into ½-inch cubes
1 (32-oz.) can V-8 juice
1 (16-oz.) can red kidney beans
1 (16-oz.) can chili beans
1 (6-oz.) can tomato paste
1 tsp. ground cumin
½ tsp. chili powder

In large skillet, brown elk in oil over medium heat, stirring to break up. Add onion, bell pepper, celery and mushrooms; continue cooking until vegetables are tender. Transfer meat and vegetables to Dutch oven or soup kettle. Add remaining ingredients and simmer about 2 hours, stirring occasionally. If you want it hotter, add more chili powder.

Arthur Van Dommelen
De Pere, WI

Cyndi's Stuffed Moose Meatloaf

1 box pork-flavor Stovetop Stuffing
2 lbs. ground moose
2 eggs, beaten
½ cup chopped onion
½ cup crushed crackers

¼ cup ketchup
1 tsp. salt
½ tsp. pepper
1 (10¾-oz.) can cream of mushroom soup
Milk (about ¾ cup)

Cook stuffing as directed on package. In large mixing bowl, combine moose, eggs, onion, crackers, ketchup, salt and pepper; mix well. In small bowl, combine soup and a half-can of milk; stir to blend. Spread half of moose mixture in baking dish. Top with prepared stuffing. Spoon half of soup mixture over stuffing. Top with remaining moose mixture; spoon remaining soup mixture over meat. Bake at 350°F for 1½ hours.

Brian Cape
Palmer, AK

Venison Potato Taco Casserole

½ lb. ground venison
1 pkg. Betty Crocker au gratin potatoes
2¼ cups boiling water

⅔ cup milk
1 cup shredded taco-seasoned cheese, divided
1 cup coarsely broken tortilla chips

In skillet, brown venison over medium heat, stirring to break up. Drain and discard excess grease. In greased casserole, mix uncooked potatoes, sauce mix from potatoes, boiling water and milk. Stir in venison and ½ cup of the cheese. Bake, uncovered, at 400°F for about 30 minutes. Sprinkle broken tortilla chips over casserole; top with remaining ½ cup shredded cheese. Return to oven and bake for 5 minutes longer, or until cheese melts. Let stand at least 2 minutes before serving.

Jim Kilgore
Bellevue, KY

Shepherd's Pie with Ground Venison

3 lbs. ground venison
1 medium onion, chopped
2 cups beef broth made from bouillon

¼ tsp. garlic powder
2 (15¼-oz.) cans whole-kernel corn, drained
6 cups mashed potatoes

In large skillet, brown venison, stirring to break up. Add chopped onion, beef broth and garlic powder; simmer until mixture thickens somewhat. Pour venison mixture into 12×10×3-inch dish. Sprinkle corn over top; do not mix. Top with mashed potatoes. Bake at 350°F for 20 minutes, or until lightly browned.

Douglas Ward
Massapequa, NY

Ground Venison Mincemeat

2 lbs. raw lean ground venison, elk or antelope
¼ lb. beef suet, ground
5 cups raisins
4 cups chopped tart apple
3 cups apple cider
2 cups currants
2 cups packed brown sugar
1½ cups white sugar
1 (8-oz.) pkg. chopped citron

½ to 1 cup coarsely chopped pecans or walnuts
¾ cup cider vinegar
Grated peels from 3 or 4 oranges
2 tsp. salt
1½ tsp. nutmeg
1 tsp. ground cloves
1 tsp. mace
1 tsp. ground allspice
¼ cup brandy or rum

In large Dutch oven or stockpot, combine all ingredients except brandy; mix well. Heat to boiling, stirring frequently. Reduce heat; cover and simmer for 2 hours, stirring occasionally. Cool. Stir in brandy. Place in pint or quart containers. Mincemeat can be stored in refrigerator for 3 or 4 days, or frozen for up to a year. You may also can the mincemeat as described on page 17.

Dennis Murdock
Grand Junction, CO

Sonny's Ground Deer Sloppy Joes

4 lbs. ground venison
2 cups minced onion
2 cups finely chopped celery
1 clove garlic, finely minced or pressed
2 (12-oz.) bottles ketchup
¼ cup Worcestershire sauce
1 T. salt
½ tsp. pepper

Heat 6-quart Dutch oven, uncovered, over medium heat for 2 to 3 minutes. Add venison, onion, celery and garlic. Cook until venison is browned, stirring to break up meat. Drain and discard excess grease. Add remaining ingredients. Cover and reduce heat to low. Cook for about 30 minutes. This makes a big batch; cool and freeze the extras in 1-pint freezer containers.

Sonny Worsham
Hendersonville, NC

West Texas Game Pie

1 to 1½ lbs. finely ground venison or elk
1 large onion, minced
1 (1¼-oz.) pkg. dry taco seasoning mix,
    or barbecue sauce or A-1 sauce to taste
2 cups mashed potatoes
½ cup shredded cheddar cheese,
    mild or sharp
Shredded lettuce
Salsa or diced fresh tomato

In large skillet, cook venison and onion until venison is browned and onion is tender, stirring to break up meat. Add taco seasoning mix and a little water, or sauce to taste, as you prefer. Stir well and cook for 5 to 10 minutes longer.

Lightly spray 9-inch glass pie dish or a large square baking dish with nonstick spray; line bottom and sides with mashed potatoes. Spoon meat mixture over potatoes. Bake at 350°F for 20 to 30 minutes; watch carefully and remove when the potatoes begin to brown on the edges. Sprinkle shredded cheddar cheese over the top and let stand 10 minutes; the cheese will melt as the dish cools off. Cut into individual pieces, and garnish with lettuce and salsa.

The Grandkids' Version

Follow recipe above, substituting crumbled corn chips for the mashed potatoes. This is the way our grandkids prefer it; we use the Hot Fritos flavor for them, but some of our friends prefer regular-flavored corn chips rather than the hot flavor. You may also add diced red or green bell peppers at the same time as the cheese, if peppers are fresh and in season.

Kenneth and Nancy White
Abilene, TX

Venison Pockets

1 small onion, diced
1 hot or mild pepper, diced
1 can sliced or diced mushrooms, drained
Vegetable oil
1 lb. ground venison
1 tube flaky refrigerator biscuits
½ lb. shredded cheese, any variety

In medium skillet, sauté onion, pepper and mushrooms in oil over medium heat. Add venison and cook until browned, stirring to break up meat. Drain and discard excess grease if necessary; set venison mixture aside.

Separate the biscuit dough into layers about ⅛ inch thick; you will get a number of layers from each biscuit. Place 2 layers into the cup of a muffin tin, pressing to seal the biscuit seams together, and line the muffin cup; the biscuit dough should extend just slightly over the top edge of the cup. Repeat until all muffin cups have been lined, reserving one biscuit layer for each cup.

Fill the pockets with the venison mixture. Sprinkle some cheese on top of the meat, being careful to keep the biscuit edge around each cup clear. Flatten remaining biscuit layers so they are big enough to cover the filled cups. Top each filled muffin cup with a flattened biscuit layer, pressing the top to seal with the biscuits at the edges. Bake as directed on the biscuit tube, usually 10 to 14 minutes at 350°F; biscuits will be golden brown when done.

This is a real favorite of mine and it is very simple to make. I hope all of my fellow hunting and cooking enthusiasts enjoy it.

Rich "Twisted" Howe
Springville, NY

**West Texas
Game Pie**

Cajun Meatloaf Surprise

3 lbs. ground venison
1½ cups seasoned breadcrumbs
1 onion, chopped
2 eggs, beaten
3 T. cajun seasoning
1 tomato, thinly sliced
¼ lb. pepper-Jack cheese, shredded

In mixing bowl, combine all ingredients except tomato and cheese. Place half the venison mixture in 9x6x2-inch baking pan. Arrange tomato slices over meat; top with shredded pepper-Jack cheese. Pack remaining venison mixture over cheese. Bake at 325°F for 1 hour, or until cooked through. To cook in microwave, use microwave-safe dish; microwave on high for 30 minutes, or according to manual.

Jim Garanin
Montague, MA

Fiery Fiesta Venison Skillet

2 lbs. ground venison
1 T. vegetable oil
1 (15-oz.) can sliced white potatoes
1 (11-oz.) can Mexican-style corn niblets
¾ cup sweet hamburger relish
1 (10-oz.) can Mexican-style diced tomatoes, drained
Salt and pepper
Garnishes: Ketchup, sliced jalapeños, hot chili sauce or habañero sauce

In large skillet, brown venison in oil over medium heat, stirring to break up. While venison is browning, warm potatoes and corn in saucepan; do not cook. When potatoes and corn are hot, drain and add to browned venison. Add relish and drained tomatoes. Cover skillet and simmer for 5 minutes. Salt and pepper to taste before serving. Individuals can mix in ketchup for a mild dish, or some sliced jalapeños and desired hot sauce for a fiery fiesta.

Herb Vroegindewey
Chesapeake, VA

Darryn's Deer Burger Quiche

½ lb. ground venison
Half of a small onion, chopped
6 eggs
Dash milk
Salt and pepper
4 slices American cheese, cut into squares,
    or ½ cup shredded cheddar cheese
1 (10-inch) pie shell

In skillet, cook venison and onion until venison is no longer pink and onion is tender, stirring to break up meat. Drain and discard excess grease. In mixing bowl, beat eggs, milk, and salt and pepper to taste. Stir in venison mixture and cheese. Pour into pie shell. Bake at 350°F for 25 minutes, or until center tests done when knife is inserted.

Darryn Warner
Bradford, OH

Swedish Meat Balls

2 lbs. ground venison
1 lb. ground pork
2 onions, finely chopped
2 cups milk
2 cups crushed rusks or other crackers
1 egg, beaten
Salt and pepper to taste
Vegetable oil, *optional*

In large mixing bowl, combine all ingredients except oil; mix well. Form into meatballs. Brown in skillet, adding a little oil if necessary; it may be necessary to brown the meatballs in several batches. Transfer browned meatballs to slow cooker. Cover and cook on low heat for 3 hours.

Randy and Sharon Russell
Burlington, IA

10-Minute Venison Chili

2 to 3 lbs. ground venison
3 onions, chopped
2 green bell peppers, chopped
Garlic salt
Hot red pepper flakes
Black pepper
2 (10¾-oz.) cans condensed tomato soup
2 (14½-oz.) cans sliced stewed tomatoes
2 (15-oz.) cans hot chili beans
Chili powder
Hot cooked rice, *optional*

In large skillet, combine venison, onions and bell peppers. Sprinkle with garlic salt, dried red pepper and black pepper to taste. Cook on high, stirring frequently to break up meat, until venison is well cooked. While venison is cooking, put soup, tomatoes and beans in another pot. Sprinkle enough chili powder over to completely cover top surface of mixture. Cook over medium heat, stirring occasionally; it's easy to alternate stirring the venison in the skillet and the soup mixture in the pot. As soon as the venison is cooked, drain and discard excess grease and add venison mixture to the pot with the soup mixture. Stir well and serve. This is great served alone or over hot cooked rice.

Joe Patterson
National City, MI

Buck Ridge Barbecue

1 lb. ground venison
1 onion, chopped
¼ tsp. garlic powder
2 T. margarine
¾ cup ketchup
2 T. prepared mustard
1 T. brown sugar
1 tsp. Worcestershire sauce
1 tsp. salt

In skillet or pot, cook venison, onion and garlic powder in margarine over medium heat until venison is no longer pink and onion is tender, stirring to break up meat. Add remaining ingredients; simmer 7 to 10 minutes.

Harold "Scottie" Scott
Cincinnati, OH

Easy Goulash

1 to 2 T. vegetable oil
1 lb. ground venison
3 cups uncooked medium egg noodles
2 cups water
1 (8-oz.) can tomato sauce
1 (1½-oz.) pkg. dry onion soup mix

In large skillet, heat oil over medium heat. Add venison and cook until lightly browned, stirring to break up. Drain and discard excess grease. Sprinkle uncooked noodles over meat. In bowl, stir together water, tomato sauce and onion soup mix. Pour tomato sauce mixture over noodles; do not stir. Cover and heat to boiling. Reduce heat and simmer for about 30 minutes, or until noodles are tender. A little water may be needed if noodles seem to be sticking. Stir and serve.

Mrs. Ron Fratrick
Franklin, WI

Enchilada Pie

2 lbs. ground venison
1 lb. regular or Italian sausage
2 (4½-oz.) cans green chilies
12 corn tortillas
2 lbs. shredded mild cheddar cheese
2 (10¾-oz.) cans cream of chicken soup
   and 1 can water
Garnishes: Chopped lettuce, chopped
   tomatoes, chopped bell peppers, chopped
   onions, taco sauce

In large skillet, brown venison and sausage, stirring to break up. Add chilies and cook for about 5 minutes longer. In deep baking dish, make layers of tortillas, meat and cheddar cheese until all is used, making sure to end up with cheese as top layer. In saucepan, heat soup and water, then pour over top of casserole, letting it go down the sides. Bake at 350°F for 1 hour. Present garnishes in individual bowls, letting each person garnish their own portion.

Robert Grimes
Dahlgren, IL

Ground Venison & Pork with Sour Cream

1 Kaiser roll	Marjoram to taste
Milk	Salt and pepper to taste
½ lb. ground venison	Breadcrumbs
½ lb. ground pork	Olive oil
1 sweet Spanish onion, chopped	Beef or venison broth, approx. ¼ cup
2 eggs, beaten	½ cup sour cream
2 cloves garlic, crushed	1 to 2 tsp. flour

Soak Kaiser roll in a little milk; squeeze dry and tear into pieces. In mixing bowl, mix venison and pork. Add Kaiser roll, onion, eggs, garlic, marjoram, and salt and pepper; mix well. Add enough breadcrumbs to make a medium firm loaf (about 2 tablespoons). Shape meat mixture into loaf, and roll in additional breadcrumbs. Heat olive oil in large oven-proof skillet, and quickly brown loaf on all sides. Add 2 to 3 tablespoons broth and bake at 350°F for 30 minutes, basting occasionally; if pan starts to dry out, add additional broth. When loaf is cooked through, transfer to heated platter. Add sour cream and flour to skillet and cook on stovetop until mixture bubbles and thickens slightly. Good side dishes include mashed potatoes (laced with chives and sour cream), along with sauerkraut and/or cranberries.

Clete Bellin
Forestville, WI

Black Bean/Salsa Venison Chili

1 lb. ground venison
1 large onion, chopped
Salt and pepper to taste
1 (15-oz.) can black beans
1 (15-oz.) can navy beans
1½ (11½-oz.) cans V-8 juice
1 (8-oz.) can diced tomato
1 cup mild salsa

In pot, brown venison over medium heat with onion, salt and pepper, stirring to break up meat. Add remaining ingredients. Heat to boiling. Reduce heat and simmer for about 30 minutes.

Tim Reid
Matthews, NC

Appetizer Venison Meatballs

2½ lbs. ground venison
½ cup seasoned croutons
1 egg, beaten
2 T. butter, melted
1 (1½-oz.) pkg. dry onion soup mix
2 (14-oz.) bottles extra spicy ketchup
1 (10-oz.) jar apple jelly
1 (8-oz.) can tomato sauce

Combine venison, croutons, egg, butter and dry soup; mix well. Shape into 1-inch meatballs. In large skillet, brown meatballs over medium-high heat. Drain on paper towels; transfer to baking dish. Stir together remaining ingredients in skillet; simmer for 10 minutes. Pour sauce over meatballs and bake at 325°F for 30 minutes.

J. Scott Westall
Roswell, GA

Mr. Bill's Favorite Hunter's Chili

3 lbs. ground venison or other big game
3 medium onions, chopped
3 medium green bell peppers, chopped
½ cup chopped celery
2 T. bacon drippings or vegetable oil
1 (28-oz.) can whole tomatoes, drained
2 (15½-oz.) cans kidney beans, undrained
1 (16-oz.) can pinto beans, undrained
2 T. dried parsley flakes

2 T. chili powder
1 tsp. salt
1 tsp. pepper
½ tsp. garlic powder or 1 clove garlic, crushed
Shredded cheddar cheese
Sour cream
Crackers

In large skillet, brown meat over medium heat, stirring to break up. Remove from heat; set aside. In Dutch oven, sauté onions, bell peppers and celery in bacon drippings until tender. Add browned meat and remaining ingredients except cheddar cheese, sour cream and crackers to Dutch oven. Simmer 1½ to 2 hours, stirring occasionally; if chili seems to be getting too dry, add some water or tomato juice. Set out bowls of cheddar cheese, sour cream and crackers to top chili.

William G. Lightbody
Ringwood, NJ

Venison Salisbury Steaks in Mushroom Gravy

5 lbs. ground venison
½ lb. ground uncooked bacon
    (a food processor works well for this)
2 medium onions, finely chopped
1 T. garlic powder
1 T. seasoned salt

1 T. smoky seasoning or 1 T. liquid smoke
1 large or 2 small eggs
¾ cup Italian-seasoned breadcrumbs
Olive oil
1 (1 lb. 12-oz.) can mushroom stems and pieces
2 (1-oz.) pkgs. dry beef gravy mix

In large bowl, combine all ingredients excepts olive oil, mushrooms and instant gravy. Hand knead until all ingredients are well mixed. Form mixture into oval patties about an inch thick and about 5 inches long. Fry in olive oil until browned on the outside but still uncooked inside. Arrange browned patties in glass or aluminum baking dish.

Drain mushrooms, retaining liquid. Add enough water to the mushroom liquid to equal the amount needed for gravy, and prepare gravy according to package directions. When gravy has thickened, add mushrooms and pour over patties. Cover dish with foil and bake at 350°F for 1 hour. Check patties with meat thermometer; center should register 165°F. Cook longer if necessary until temperature is reached.

James Wiggins
Rome, OH

Mr. Bill's Favorite Hunter's Chili

UPLAND
BIRDS

Oven-Fried Quail

Oven-Fried Quail

    6 whole dressed quail
    ½ cup herb stuffing mix, crushed
    ⅓ cup grated Parmesan cheese
    2 T. finely chopped green onion
    ⅓ cup butter, melted

Spilt quail down the back and flatten. Combine crushed stuffing mix, Parmesan cheese and green onion. Dip quail in melted butter, then coat with stuffing mixture. Arrange in 13×9×2-inch baking dish. Bake at 350°F for 30 minutes if quail are small; for larger quail add 10 to 15 minutes. Quail is done when meat can easily be removed from the bone.

Ron and Mary Lange
Marquette, MI

Turkey Parmesan

    Boneless, skinless breast halves from
      1 wild turkey
    Beaten egg
    Breadcrumbs
    Vegetable oil
    Tomato sauce
    Shredded or sliced mozzarella cheese

Steam turkey breast until meat is white, then set aside until cool. Slice into slabs ½ to ¾ inch thick. Coat slices with beaten egg, then roll in breadcrumbs. Fry until golden brown in hot oil. Layer in baking dish, alternating meat, tomato sauce and mozzarella cheese. Cover dish with foil and bake at 350°F for 30 minutes.

Michael A. Carrano
Hannacroix, NY

Slow-Cooked Dove

    2 slices bacon, chopped
    10 or more large fresh white mushrooms
    3 medium onions, coarsely chopped
    12 to 14 skinless dove breasts, bone-in
    1 cup flour, approx.
    1 (10¾-oz.) can cream of mushroom soup
    1 (10¾-oz.) can cream of celery soup
    1 cup chicken broth or other poultry stock
    ¼ cup dry vermouth or dry white wine
    2 bay leaves
    ¼ tsp. crumbled dried basil leaves
    ¼ tsp. dried dill weed
    ¼ tsp. garlic powder
    10 whole peppercorns
    Salt to taste
    Hot cooked noodles

In large skillet, cook bacon until crisp. Use slotted spoon to transfer bacon to paper towel-lined plate, reserving bacon drippings. Pat excess grease from bacon and transfer to small dish; cover and refrigerate until serving time. Sauté mushrooms and onions in bacon drippings; use slotted spoon to transfer vegetables to slow cooker. Coat dove breasts with flour and brown in bacon drippings; transfer dove breasts to slow cooker. Add remaining ingredients except noodles to slow cooker. Cover and cook on high for 4 to 6 hours, or on low if a longer cooking time is desired. Just before serving, re-warm bacon in microwave or small skillet. Serve doves over hot cooked noodles; garnish with bacon.

Note: Dove can sometimes have a strong odor when raw. This doesn't mean the meat is rotten; it just smells different. Although this odor vanishes when the dove is cooked, it can be reduced ahead of time by refrigerating the breasts overnight in buttermilk; drain and discard the buttermilk the next day and rinse dove breasts before proceeding.

C.T. Rybka
Port Tobacco, MD

Wild Turkey & Venison Meatballs

2 lbs. ground wild turkey leg and thigh meat
2 lbs. ground venison
2 cups Italian-seasoned breadcrumbs
2 cups grated Parmesan cheese
¾ cup chopped fresh parsley
½ cup chopped onion
½ cup chopped green bell pepper
2 T. chopped garlic

2 T. Italian seasoning
2 T. salt
1 T. pepper
4 eggs
½ cup chilled red wine
1 stick butter (8 T.)
½ cup olive oil

In large mixing bowl, combine all ingredients except eggs, wine, butter and olive oil; mix well. In a small bowl, beat eggs and wine together lightly, then add to meat mixture and mix well. If the mixture seems a little loose, add a little more breadcrumbs; if it seems too dry, add a little more wine and egg. Cover and refrigerate for 30 minutes.

When ready to cook, roll meat mixture into 4-ounce balls; you should have about 24. In large, heavy skillet, melt butter in olive oil. Brown meatballs on one side for about 5 minutes, then turn and brown second side. It may be necessary to brown meatballs in 2 batches, using additional butter and oil. When all of the meatballs are browned, drain on absorbent paper.

The meatballs can now be frozen for later use. You may also add them to your favorite tomato sauce and simmer for about 1 hour. Or, bake them at 350°F for 15 minutes and enjoy them with barbecue sauce, hot sauce or your favorite gravy. This is the perfect way to use turkey thighs and leg meat.

Michael Gordon
Venice, FL

Woodcock Imperial

    8 woodcock, cut into halves
    1 cup flour
    1 T. salt
    1 tsp. white pepper
    3 T. butter
    1 (10¾-oz.) can cream of mushroom soup
    ⅓ cup sour cream
    ¼ cup red wine
    1 cup fresh mushrooms, sliced

Dredge woodcock in flour that has been mixed with the salt and pepper. In large skillet, brown woodcock in butter over medium heat. Transfer browned woodcock to baking dish. In small bowl, blend together soup, sour cream and wine. Pour over woodcock in baking dish. Top with sliced mushrooms. Cover dish and bake at 325°F for 1 to 2 hours, or until woodcock are tender.

Keith Sutton
Alexander, AR

Pheasant Garlic Chunks

    2 pheasants, cut into small chunks
    Flour seasoned with salt, pepper and
        seasoning salt to taste
    Vegetable oil
    1 (6-oz.) jar crushed garlic

Dredge pheasant chunks in seasoned flour. Heat oil and 1 tablespoon crushed garlic in skillet. Add pheasant chunks, a few at a time, and fry until golden brown and cooked through. You will need to change oil and garlic frequently, as the garlic will burn. Serve pheasant chunks with toothpicks as appetizer.

Sally Shaffer
Dixon, SD

Glazed Pheasant

    1 pheasant, cut into halves
        (this also works well with grouse)
    2 T. peach or apricot preserves
    1 tsp. Worcestershire sauce
    1 tsp. tomato paste
    1 tsp. minced garlic

Place pheasant halves in baking dish. In small bowl, combine remaining ingredients and brush generously over pheasant. Bake at 350°F for 30 to 40 minutes. Just before serving, brush pheasant with any remaining glaze and place under broiler to brown.

Defort Bailey
Irvine, KY

Roasted Honey Pheasant

    1 whole dressed pheasant
    ¾ cup honey
    ½ cup creamy peanut butter
    2 T. cider vinegar
    2 T. soy sauce
    ½ tsp. sea salt or regular salt

Place pheasant in roasting pan. In medium saucepan, stir together remaining ingredients. Cook over low heat until peanut butter melts, stirring frequently. Pour sauce over pheasant, turning to coat. Cover and refrigerate overnight.

Bake at 350°F for 1 hour, basting frequently with drippings.

Michael Fair
Orange Park, FL

Pheasant & Bleu Cheese Roulade

Boneless, skinless breast halves from 2 pheasants
6 oz. bleu cheese
4 T. butter (half of a stick), softened
12 slices bacon
Olive oil or vegetable oil

½ cup red wine
½ cup game stock
Salt and pepper
1 tsp. cornstarch blended with 2 tsp. cold water
Watercress for garnish

Flatten pheasant breasts with meat mallet or rolling pin. In small bowl, blend together bleu cheese and butter; spread cheese mixture evenly over one side of each pheasant breast. Roll breasts up and wrap each with 3 slices bacon. Secure with wooden toothpicks. Heat small amount of oil in skillet and brown rolls evenly on all sides. Pour off excess grease if necessary, then add wine, stock, and salt and pepper to taste. Heat to boiling. Reduce heat, cover and simmer for 30 to 40 minutes, turning rolls occasionally. Transfer rolls to heated serving platter and remove toothpicks; cover loosely to keep warm. Add cornstarch slurry to skillet and cook, stirring constantly, until sauce bubbles and thickens. Spoon a little sauce over the pheasant rolls and garnish with watercress. Serve remaining sauce on the side.

John A. Phillips
Wilmette, IL

Amy & Gary's Gameland Spaghetti

3 lbs. bone-in game bird, or 1 lb. boneless
8 oz. uncooked thin spaghetti
4 T. butter (half of a stick)
¼ cup flour
1 cup half-and-half
1 cup grated Parmesan cheese, plus
    additional for garnish
1 cup mayonnaise (low- or no-fat works fine)

1 cup sour cream (low- or no-fat works fine)
⅓ cup white wine
2 T. lemon juice
1 tsp. dry mustard
½ to 1 tsp. garlic powder
¼ to ½ tsp. ground cayenne pepper
Paprika

Boil game bird until cooked. Transfer to plate, reserving broth. When meat is cool enough to handle, tear into small pieces, discarding bones, and place in large mixing bowl. Reserve 1 cup broth, then cook spaghetti in remaining broth. Drain spaghetti and transfer to mixing bowl. In saucepan, melt butter over medium-low heat, then blend in flour and cook until smooth and bubbly, stirring constantly. Gradually add half-and-half and reserved 1 cup broth, stirring constantly, and cook until thickened and bubbly. Stir in remaining ingredients except paprika. Add to mixing bowl and stir well to combine. Transfer to 13×9×2-inch baking dish. Sprinkle with paprika and Parmesan cheese. Bake at 350°F for 30 to 40 minutes.

Variation: Sauté 8 ounces sliced mushrooms in a little butter, and add to other ingredients in mixing bowl. Proceed as directed.

Gary Wells
Portales, NM

Pheasant & Bleu
Cheese Roulade

Ptarmigan with Pecan Dressing

½ cup white grape juice
¼ cup raisins
¼ cup chopped onions
4 T. butter or margarine (half of a stick)
2 cups crumbled cornmeal muffins
2 eggs, lightly beaten
¾ cup chopped pecans

½ tsp. salt
¼ tsp. poultry seasoning
Dash pepper
4 whole dressed ptarmigan
Parsley for garnish
Hot cooked wild rice

Combine grape juice and raisins in small bowl. Cover and refrigerate for 8 to 10 hours. When ready to cook, in small skillet sauté onions in butter over medium-low heat until tender. Transfer onions to mixing bowl. Add raisins with grape juice, crumbled muffins, eggs, pecans, salt, poultry seasoning and pepper; mix well. Stuff ptarmigan with mixture; place stuffed ptarmigan in 12×9-inch baking dish. Bake at 350°F for 1¼ hours. Garnish with parsley; serve with wild rice.

Joe and Becky Stahl
Fort Richardson, AK

Scott's Pheasant in Mushroom Sauce

½ cup flour
½ tsp. salt
½ tsp. paprika
½ tsp. pepper
2 pheasants, cut into serving pieces with breasts kept intact
¼ cup vegetable oil
½ cup brandy

1 clove garlic, minced
½ tsp. crumbled dried thyme leaves
½ tsp. seasoned salt
1 (10¾-oz.) can cream of mushroom soup
1 (4-oz.) can sliced mushrooms, undrained
½ cup milk
½ cup sherry
½ cup chopped fresh parsley

In shallow dish, mix flour, salt, paprika and pepper. Dredge pheasant pieces in flour mixture. In Dutch oven or large pan, brown pheasant pieces on all sides in oil over medium heat. Transfer pheasant pieces to plate; set aside. Pour off and discard leftover oil. Add brandy to Dutch oven, stirring to loosen browned bits. Cook for about a minute to deglaze Dutch oven. Add garlic, thyme and seasoned salt, and cook for a few seconds, stirring constantly. Add remaining ingredients, stirring to mix. Return pheasant pieces to Dutch oven. Cover and bake at 350°F for 1½ hours, or until tender. To serve, transfer pheasant pieces to heated serving platter and pour gravy over pheasant.

This recipe may also be used for game hens; reduce cooking time to 1 hour.

Scott Hansen
Ogden, UT

Pheasant Limone

Boneless, skinless breast halves from
   2 pheasants
¼ cup olive oil
½ cup Italian-seasoned bread crumbs
2 T. grated Parmesan cheese
2 T. butter
1 tsp. flour
½ cup pheasant stock or chicken broth
2 T. dry white wine
2 T. lemon juice
½ cup sliced mushrooms
6 capers

Combine pheasant breasts and olive oil in re-sealable plastic bag and refrigerate several hours or overnight, turning bag occasionally. In wide, shallow dish, mix bread crumbs and Parmesan cheese. Dredge pheasant breasts in bread crumb mixture. Oven broil 6 inches from heat for about 5 minutes per side; do not overcook. Transfer to heated serving platter; cover loosely and keep warm.

In saucepan, melt butter over medium-low heat, then blend in flour and cook until smooth and bubbly, stirring constantly. Add stock, wine and lemon juice and cook until thickened and bubbly. Add mushrooms and capers and cook for a minute or two. Serve sauce over hot pheasant breasts.

Janice Anderson
St. Louis, MO

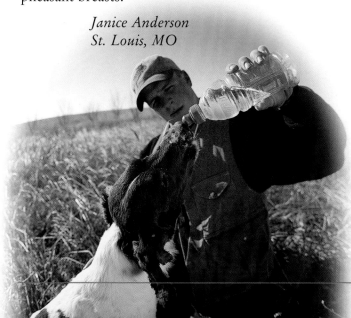

Ron's Crock Pot Doves

8 to 10 whole dressed doves
Vegetable oil
1 (10¾-oz.) can cream of mushroom soup
4 or 5 slices bacon, chopped
¼ cup finely chopped onion
¼ cup red wine
½ cup uncooked rice
2 cloves garlic, finely chopped
2 T. hot sauce
½ tsp. salt
½ tsp. pepper
¼ tsp. crumbled dried oregano leaves

In skillet, sear doves briefly in a little oil; transfer doves to slow cooker. Add remaining ingredients and mix well. Cover and cook on low for 4 to 6 hours, stirring occasionally.

Dr. Ron Paque
Boerne, TX

Au Gratin Pheasant

Skinless breast halves from 4 pheasants,
   boneless or bone-in
8 slices Swiss cheese, or 2 cups shredded
   Swiss cheese
1 (10¾-oz.) can cream of chicken soup
¼ cup dry white wine
2 cups seasoned breadcrumbs
⅓ cup butter, melted

Arrange breasts in shallow baking pan. Place 2 slices cheese on each breast. In mixing bowl, stir together soup and wine; spoon mixture evenly over each breast. Sprinkle breadcrumbs evenly over the top. Drizzle melted butter evenly over crumbs. Bake, uncovered, at 350°F for 1 hour.

Kris Gulick
Cedar Rapids, IA

Grilled Grouse in Foil

Breasts and legs from 2 grouse
Salt water solution
Large sheet of heavy-duty foil
2 T. butter
1 tsp. salt, or to taste
Black pepper

1 green bell pepper, sliced
1 red bell pepper, sliced
1 slice onion
½ cup white wine
¼ cup vegetable oil

Bone grouse breasts, discarding bones. Soak breasts and legs in salt water for about an hour to draw out any blood. Arrange breasts and legs side by side on shiny side of foil. Place pats of butter on grouse pieces. Sprinkle with salt and pepper to taste. Top with pepper and onion slices. Fold edges of foil up slightly to form a rim, and add wine and oil to packet. Roll-fold top of foil together, then roll-fold side in to form a neat, well-sealed packet. Place on preheated grill and cover the grill. Cook for about 35 minutes, then check for tenderness. It should be ready at this point, but may need a little additional cooking time if the grouse were older. The oil and butter keep the meat juicy in this recipe.

Ed Sutton
Delton, MI

"Grouse are exciting birds to hunt on a crisp fall morning, or any time for that matter. Your dog goes on point in a stand of aspen and bracken fern. She creeps forward a bit, and you know the bird is moving. Slowly you move in, shotgun at ready, anticipating a thunderous flash at any moment. Your heart beats a little faster. Your eyes search the ground ahead of the dog; though you seldom see the bird, still you look. When it finally happens, a blur of brown explodes in front of you, leaving you unhinged for a moment even though you knew it was coming. Somehow you throw the gun to your shoulder and fire, and you hear that wonderful thump as the bird hits the ground. Your dog returns with the plump, brown-feathered bird in her mouth, looking as proud as you are about what you and she have accomplished. If you're lucky and shoot straight, you may add a couple more to the day's bag.

"That's not where the joy of grouse hunting ends, not at all. If you're fortunate enough to take a brace of birds you have some fine eating ahead. The white meat of a ruffed grouse is tender, juicy and delicious if prepared properly, and will leave you wanting more. Here's my favorite way of preparing this wonderful bird."

—Ed Sutton

Grilled Grouse
in Foil

Quail in Mushroom Gravy

¾ cup flour, divided
1 tsp. salt
½ tsp. pepper
6 whole dressed quail
1 stick butter or margarine (8 T.)
½ lb. fresh mushrooms, sliced
2 cups chicken broth
2 tsp. minced fresh thyme, leaves or ¾ tsp.
   crumbled dried thyme leaves
Hot cooked noodles, *optional*

In shallow dish, mix together ½ cup of the flour with the salt and pepper. Dredge quail in seasoned flour. In large skillet, melt butter over medium heat and brown quail on all sides. Transfer browned quail to ungreased 2½-quart baking dish. Sauté mushrooms until tender in drippings remaining in skillet. Add remaining ¼ cup flour to skillet, stirring to make smooth paste. Add broth and thyme to skillet, stirring constantly. Heat to boiling and cook, stirring constantly, until thickened, about 1 minute. Pour mushroom sauce over quail. Cover and bake at 350°F for 40 to 50 minutes, or until quail are tender and juices run clear. Serve over noodles if desired.

Frank Bruno
Dubois, WY

Dad's Italian Barbecued Bird

8 whole dressed small game birds of your
   choice: dove, quail, chukar or grouse
½ cup Italian salad dressing
1 T. paprika
1 tsp. rubbed sage leaves
½ tsp. garlic powder
Salt and pepper to taste
1 lb. bacon

Marinate birds in Italian salad dressing overnight. When ready to cook, pat dry and season with paprika, sage, garlic powder, and salt and pepper. Wrap each bird with bacon slices; if you use more than 1 slice of bacon for each bird, match the seams on the same side. Place birds on medium-hot grill, with the bacon seam down. Cover and grill for 15 minutes. Turn and grill for 15 minutes longer. Test the bird with a fork; if not tender, continue cooking for up to 15 minutes longer.

When you barbecue these smaller birds, they tend to be a little on the dry side. This recipe will definitely fix that.

Michael Fair
Orange Park, FL

Baked Partridge in Port

3 or 4 whole dressed Hungarian partridge or ruffed grouse, or 6 quail
Salt and pepper
6 to 8 slices bacon
3 whole oranges, washed and thinly sliced
3 large ribs celery, sliced ½ inch thick
2 cups chicken broth or consommé
1 cup port wine

Sprinkle birds inside and out with salt and pepper. Wrap 1 or 2 slices bacon around each bird, covering legs to hold close to body; secure with wooden toothpicks. Place in roasting pan and add remaining ingredients. Bake at 375°F for 30 minutes, or until birds are tender. Remove bacon, strain gravy and pour over birds.

Clete Bellin
Forestville, WI

Birds in a Breeze

1 apple, peeled and sliced ½ inch thick
Boneless breast halves from 1 or 2 pheasants, or equivalent in turkey breast meat
3 or 4 slices bacon

Spread apple slices in slow cooker. Arrange pheasant breasts over apples; top with bacon. Cover and cook on medium for 3 to 4 hours, depending on the amount of meat; check to see that the meat is completely cooked by slicing it open. Good with wild rice.

This method produces meat that is very tender, and has all its natural juices intact as well as the flavor of the apples and bacon. For such a simple dish, you won't believe how good it can be.

Rich Howe
Springville, NY

Pheasant & Rice Bake

1 (1½-oz.) pkg. dry onion soup mix
1 cup uncooked rice
1 pheasant, cut into serving pieces
1 (10¾-oz.) can cream of chicken soup
1 (10¾-oz.) soup can milk
1 (2.8-oz.) can French-fried onion rings

Sprinkle onion soup mix into buttered 2-quart casserole. Sprinkle rice over soup mix. Arrange pheasant pieces evenly in casserole. In mixing bowl, stir together cream of chicken soup with milk; pour over pheasant. Cover and bake at 350°F for 1 hour 15 minutes. Uncover and sprinkle with onion rings; bake for 15 minutes longer.

Darrell Whitman
Cody, WY

Fried Turkey Breast

Boneless, skinless breast halves from 1 wild turkey
1 quart buttermilk
3 cups flour
1 T. Cajun seasoning, or more to taste
1½ to 2 cups shortening

Cut turkey breast 1 inch thick across the grain. Pound with meat mallet to tenderize. Place in glass dish; cover with buttermilk. Cover and refrigerate for 4 to 6 hours. Remove turkey from buttermilk; discard buttermilk. In shallow dish, mix flour and seasoning. Dredge each piece of turkey in seasoned flour. Melt shortening in cast-iron skillet or pot, and fry turkey pieces until golden brown. You can make a cream gravy from the drippings if desired.

Mary Greider
Houston, TX

Turkey Chowder

Turkey Chowder

1 medium onion, chopped
3 T. margarine or butter
2 cups diced cooked turkey meat
2 cups turkey broth or chicken broth
1½ cups diced potatoes
1 cup diced carrots
½ cup diced celery with leaves
2 T. flour
2½ cups milk
1 tsp. salt
Dash of pepper

In large saucepan, sauté onion in butter until tender. Add diced turkey, broth, potatoes, carrots and celery. Cover saucepan and simmer until vegetables are tender.

In small bowl, combine flour with enough milk to make a smooth paste. Add to remaining milk. Stir into saucepan with salt and pepper. Simmer until slightly thickened.

Carl Bartelt
Hillsboro, WI

Dove Stew

10 to 12 whole dressed doves
3 ribs celery, diced
2 carrots, diced
1 medium onion, diced
1 (14½-oz.) can tomato sauce
2½ cups water
2 medium potatoes, 1 diced and 1 grated
1 bell pepper, diced
4 chicken bouillon cubes
Salt and pepper to taste

In saucepan, combine doves, celery, carrots, onion, tomato sauce and water. Cover and simmer for 30 minutes. Remove doves and set aside until cool enough to handle. Remove meat from bones; discard bones. Return dove meat to saucepan. Add potatoes, bell pepper and bouillon cubes. Simmer for 30 minutes longer, replacing liquid that cooks away. Just before serving, add salt and pepper to taste. Serve with hot buttered cornbread.

Jack Ussery
Corpus Christi, TX

Pheasant in Almond Cream Sauce

2 whole or cut-up pheasants
Italian-seasoned bread crumbs, finely ground
Grated Parmesan cheese
Vegetable oil or olive oil

1 (10¾-oz.) can cream of mushroom soup
1 cup sour cream
⅔ cup white wine
4 oz. slivered almonds

Cut up pheasants into pieces if necessary. Fillet breast portions from bones; discard breastbones. Combine bread crumbs and Parmesan cheese on a plate and dredge pheasant pieces in crumb mixture. In skillet, brown pheasant pieces lightly in a little cooking oil; brown in two batches if necessary to avoid crowding. Transfer browned pheasant pieces to glass baking dish.

In saucepan, combine soup, sour cream and white wine and heat over low heat until warm. Pour soup mixture over pheasant pieces and bake at 350°F for 30 minutes. Sprinkle almond pieces over the top 5 to 7 minutes before the pheasant is done.

Mike Read
Pearland, TX

Upland Bird Wild Rice Casserole

½ lb. pork sausage
½ lb. mushrooms, sliced
3 ribs celery, chopped
1 large onion, chopped
½ cup flour
½ tsp. salt
¼ tsp. pepper

1 lb. quail, pheasant or other upland bird
1 cup wild rice, soaked overnight and drained
1 (10¾-oz.) can cream of mushroom soup
1 (15-oz.) can Chinese vegetables, drained
1 cup water
½ cup soy sauce

In large skillet, cook pork sausage, mushrooms, celery and onion over medium heat, stirring to break up meat, until cooked sausage is cooked through and vegetables are tender. With slotted spoon, transfer sausage and vegetables to slow cooker, reserving drippings. Combine flour, salt and pepper; dredge birds in seasoned flour. Brown birds in sausage drippings. Add birds and remaining ingredients to slow cooker with vegetables and sausage. Cover and cook on low for 3 to 4 hours, or until rice and meat is tender; add more water if necessary. This may also be baked in covered casserole at 350°F.

Bruce Williams
Silver City, NM

Grouse Baked in Sour Cream

½ cup flour
1 tsp. crumbled dried thyme leaves, or
   ½ tsp. crumbled dried rosemary leaves
Salt and pepper
4 grouse, cut into halves
1 stick butter (8 T.), divided

½ lb. mushrooms, sliced
4 shallots
2 cups sour cream, at room temperature
½ cup chicken broth
1 tsp. plum jelly
Hot cooked wild rice

Combine flour with thyme, and salt and pepper to taste. Dredge grouse in seasoned flour. In large oven-proof skillet, brown grouse in 6 tablespoons of the butter over medium heat. Transfer browned grouse to dish; set aside. In same skillet, melt remaining 2 tablespoons butter. Sauté mushrooms and shallots until mushrooms are tender. Add sour cream, chicken broth and plum jelly to skillet, stirring to blend. Return grouse to skillet; cover and bake at 350°F for about 1 hour. Serve with wild rice.

Frank Bruno
Dubois, WY

Roasted Wild Turkey

10- to 15-lb. whole dressed wild turkey
2 large apples, quartered
6 to 8 medium red potatoes, quartered
2 lbs. baby carrots
2 medium onions, sliced
2 cups water
1½ tsp. seasoned salt
1 tsp. plain salt
1 tsp. pepper
½ cup maple syrup
¼ cup French salad dressing
¼ cup barbecue sauce
2 T. ketchup
2 T. steak sauce
1 T. lemon juice

Place turkey on rack in roasting pan; place apples in turkey cavity. Place potatoes, carrots and onions around turkey. Pour water over vegetables. In small bowl, combine seasoned salt, salt and pepper; rub over turkey. Combine remaining ingredients; brush over turkey. Cover roasting pan and bake at 325°F for 3½ hours, or until thigh meat reads 180°F when tested with meat thermometer. Turkey may be uncovered for last 30 minutes of roasting if additional browning is desired.

Don Wallis
Citrus Heights, CA

Pheasant Cacciatore

1 pheasant, cut into serving pieces
Flour seasoned with salt and pepper
½ cup olive oil
3 cups fresh or canned tomato, crushed roughly
1 onion, chopped
3 cloves garlic, chopped
½ of (6-oz.) can of tomato paste
Salt and pepper to taste
½ tsp. hot red pepper flakes
2 T. chopped fresh oregano leaves
2 T. chopped fresh flat-leaf parsley
Hot cooked spaghetti or rice

Dredge pheasant pieces in seasoned flour. In Dutch oven, brown pheasant on all sides in oil over medium heat. Add remaining ingredients except spaghetti to Dutch oven. Simmer for 20 to 30 minutes, or until pheasant is cooked through. Remove pheasant from Dutch oven and set aside; cook sauce for 1 hour longer. Before serving, return pheasant to sauce and cook until pheasant is heated through. Serve over spaghetti or rice.

Ken Colgan
Flushing, NY

Sharptail Rosemary

4 sharptail grouse or ruffed grouse,
  or 2 pheasants
3 cups cold water
1½ cup white wine, divided
2 T. sea salt
4 T. butter (half of a stick) or olive oil
1 cup sliced mushrooms
2 or 3 cloves garlic, minced
2 T. fresh rosemary leaves
2 cups half-and-half
2 cups heavy cream
3 to 4 T. julienned sun-dried tomatoes
2 tsp. freshly ground black pepper
1½ tsp. salt
2 T. chopped fresh parsley
Cooked wild rice pilaf

Bone all meat from grouse and cut into generous bite-sized chunks or strips; discard bones or use to make stock for another recipe. In large bowl or casserole dish, combine grouse meat, water, 1 cup of the wine and the sea salt. Cover and refrigerate overnight.

When ready to cook, drain grouse meat, discarding marinade. Melt butter in large skillet over medium heat. Add grouse, mushrooms, garlic, rosemary and the remaining ½ cup wine and sauté until grouse is cooked through. Add half-and-half, cream, sun-dried tomatoes, pepper and salt and simmer until slightly thickened, about 20 minutes. Stir in parsley, and serve over wild rice pilaf.

Ineke Leer
Walker, MN

Dove Pie

2½ to 3 cups diced boneless uncooked
  breast meat from dove, pheasant or grouse
2 T. vegetable oil
1 potato, cut into ½-inch cubes
1½ cups frozen peas-and-carrots mix, thawed
½ cup thinly sliced celery
½ cup chopped onion
2 frozen pie shells, thawed
1 (12-oz.) jar chicken gravy

In skillet, brown dove meat in oil over medium heat. Transfer to mixing bowl. Add potato, and pea-carrot mix. Cook for 5 minutes, stirring occasionally. Add celery and onion. Cook for 3 minutes longer, stirring occasionally. Transfer vegetables to mixing bowl with browned meat. Stir well, and pour into one of the pie shells. Pour gravy over the meat and vegetables. Top with second pie crust, pinching edges of crust together well. Cut a small hole, or several slits, in top crust. Bake at 375°F for 30 to 35 minutes.

Ed Russell
Oconta, WI

Wild Turkey Dip

2 cups chopped cooked wild turkey meat
1 (16-oz.) container sour cream
1 (8-oz.) block cream cheese, softened
2 cups shredded cheese
1 cup mayonnaise
1½ (1½-oz.) pkgs. french onion soup mix

In medium bowl, combine all ingredients and mix well. Chill to blend flavors; stir again before serving. Serve with corn chips or potato chips.

Jayme Schertz
Menosha, WI

Sharptail
Rosemary

Barbecued Grouse or Quail

2 whole dressed grouse or 4 quail
1 clove garlic
¼ tsp. salt
Leafy tops from 2 ribs celery
2 small onions, quartered
2 to 4 sprigs fresh parsley
1 whole lemon, well washed
¼ cup olive oil
1 tsp. onion juice
¼ tsp. Tabasco sauce
¼ tsp. crumbled dried thyme leaves

Rinse birds in cold water; pat dry. Rub inside and out with garlic and salt. Stuff birds with celery tops, onions and parsley sprigs, and place on rack in roasting pan. Grate lemon rind and add to large jar. Squeeze juice from lemon and add to jar. Add oil, onion juice, Tabasco sauce and thyme to jar. Seal jar tightly and shake well. Brush some of the lemon sauce over the birds. Cover roaster and bake at 375°F for 40 minutes, basting with lemon sauce every 10 minutes.

David Miller
Harriman, NY

Pheasant Cutlets Supreme

2 quarts cold water
1 cup wine vinegar or cider vinegar
1 clove garlic, cut into small pieces
Bone-in breast from 1 pheasant
Crumbled dried oregano leaves
Salt and pepper
1 egg, beaten
Seasoned breadcrumbs
Vegetable oil
Lemon juice
Garlic powder

In nonaluminum bowl, combine water, vinegar and garlic. Add pheasant breast; sprinkle surface of water with oregano, salt and pepper. Cover and refrigerate overnight. The next day, fillet breast meat from bone. Separate out the small cutlet underneath each breast half, then cut breast halves into 2 cutlets each, so you have 4 large cutlets and 2 smaller cutlets. Dip cutlets in egg, then into breadcrumbs. In lightly greased skillet, cook cutlets in a little oil until golden brown; while cutlets are browning, sprinkle with a few drops of lemon juice, and some garlic powder, salt and pepper to taste. After cutlets are brown, add ½ inch water to skillet. Cover skillet; reduce heat and simmer for 1 hour. The cutlets will be moist and tasty.

Anthony De Franco
Patterson, NJ

Smothered Game Bird Breasts

Marinade:
¼ cup red wine vinegar
2 tsp. sugar
1 tsp. crushed fennel seed
½ tsp. salt
¼ tsp. rubbed sage leaves

Boneless, skinless breast halves from
   4 game birds
2 T. olive oil
1 large onion, halved and thinly sliced
2 tsp. sugar
1 cup low-sodium defatted chicken broth
1 T. flour
1 carrot, cut into thin strips
1 red bell pepper, cut into thin strips
1 large white mushroom, thinly sliced
¼ cup red wine vinegar
½ tsp. black pepper

In small bowl, stir together marinade ingredients. Place breasts in resealable plastic bag. Add marinade; seal bag and turn to coat. Refrigerate overnight, turning occasionally.

When ready to cook, heat oil in large non-stick skillet over medium heat. Add onions and sugar; cook for 5 minutes, or until onion starts to brown, stirring occasionally. Add broth and cook for 5 to 8 minutes longer. Stir in remaining ingredients. Cook, stirring occasionally, until onions are tender, about 12 minutes.

Heat broiler. Drain breasts and place on broiler pan; broil about 4 inches from heat for about 6 minutes per side, or until cooked through. To serve, place breasts on warm plate and spoon onion mixture around meat.

Robert W. Dixon
Sandpoint, ID

Thai Onion-Turkey Noodles

8 oz. boneless turkey breast, cut into
   ½-inch strips
2 T. soy sauce, divided
3 T. vegetable oil, divided
2 sweet medium Spanish onions, cut
   into ¼-inch wedges
¾ cup red bell pepper strips, ¼ inch wide
¾ cup green bell pepper strips, ¼ inch wide
2 tsp. minced fresh gingerroot
1 tsp. minced garlic
½ tsp. hot red pepper flakes
1 cup chicken broth
1 T. cornstarch blended with ¼ cup cold
   water
8 oz. medium-wide egg noodles, cooked
   and drained
1 tsp. Oriental sesame oil
Chopped fresh cilantro for garnish

Toss turkey strips with 1 tablespoon of the soy sauce. In wok or large skillet, heat 1 tablespoon of the oil over high heat. Add turkey; cook and stir until just cooked through. With slotted spoon, transfer turkey to bowl; set aside. Add remaining 2 tablespoons oil to wok. Add onion, and red and green bell peppers; cook and stir for 2 minutes. Add gingerroot, garlic and red pepper to wok; cook and stir for 2 to 3 minutes longer, or until vegetables are tender-crisp. Stir broth and remaining tablespoon of soy sauce into wok; heat to boiling. Gradually add cornstarch slurry, cooking and stirring until mixture thickens and bubbles. Add noodles, sesame oil and cooked turkey, tossing and cooking until all ingredients are heated. Garnish with chopped cilantro.

Felicia Randall
Traverse City, MI

WATERFOWL

Roast Goose

Flour
1 large oven roasting bag
1 cup apple juice
½ cup chopped apple
½ cup chopped onion
6- to 8-lb. whole dressed wild goose
1 T. butter, softened
1 tsp. rubbed sage leaves
Salt and pepper
1 apple, cored and quartered
1 onion, peeled and quartered
⅓ cup currant jelly

Sprinkle flour into oven roasting bag as directed by manufacturer; twist top and shake to distribute. Place bag in 2-inch-deep roasting pan. Add apple juice, chopped apple and chopped onion to roasting bag and turn to mix. Rub goose cavity with butter. Add sage to cavity, and sprinkle with salt and pepper to taste. Place apple and onion quarters in goose cavity. Tie goose legs together, and place goose in roasting bag. Close and seal bag, then cut several slits in top of bag. Bake at 325°F for 2½ hours, or until goose is tender. Transfer goose to serving platter; cover loosely and set aside.

Pour roasting liquid into large measuring cup. Skim and discard excess fat. Pour measured liquid into saucepan. Whisk in 2 tablespoons flour for each cup of liquid you measured. Add currant jelly. Heat to boiling, stirring constantly, and cook until thickened and bubbly. Serve the gravy over the goose.

We've had wonderful results when roasting a goose in an oven bag. The bag holds the moisture so the meat does not get dry, and the taste of the roasted goose is incomparable!

Ron and Mary Lange
Marquette, WI

Mallard Supreme

1 wild duck, cut into serving pieces
Flour seasoned with salt and pepper
1 stick margarine (8 T.)
1 large can condensed milk

Roll duck pieces in seasoned flour. In roaster or heavy pan, melt margarine over medium heat and brown floured duck pieces on all sides. Pour condensed milk over browned duck. Cover and bake at 375°F until duck is tender; if it begins to get dry, add a small amount of water. To serve, discard the condensed milk and serve only the meat. Very different, rich and tasty.

Paul J. Woychik
Arcadia, WI

Saucy Apple Goose

1 whole dressed wild goose
2 apples, cored, peeled and sliced
1 (14-oz.) can applesauce
½ cup corn syrup
¼ cup currant jelly
1 tsp. cinnamon
1 tsp. nutmeg

Place goose in roasting pan. Add apples to cavity. Bake at 350°F, allowing 20 to 25 minutes per pound. As soon as you put the goose in the oven, combine remaining ingredients in a saucepan and heat for a few minutes, then baste goose frequently with the applesauce mixture. Serve remaining sauce over carved goose.

John Hawryluk
Moncton, NB

Roast Goose

Crock Pot Duck & Dressing

1 cup chopped onion
1 cup chopped celery
1 stick butter (8 T.)
1 pan cornbread, crumbled
6 slices bread, crumbled
1/4 lb. crackers, crumbled
2 tsp. chopped fresh thyme or sage
4 to 5 cups broth
4 eggs, beaten
1/2 cup milk
1/2 tsp. baking powder
3 to 4 cups bite-sized pieces cooked wild duck meat

In skillet, sauté onion and celery in butter until tender. While vegetables are cooking, combine crumbled cornbread, sliced bread and crackers in very large mixing bowl. Pour cooked vegetables and thyme over breads, and toss together. Add enough broth to mixture to moisten, then add eggs and mix together well. Add milk, baking powder and as much of the remaining broth as needed to make a very moist mixture; it should be slushy enough to pour. Stir in duck, and pack mixture lightly into 5-quart slow cooker. Cover and cook on high for 1 hour. Reduce heat to low and cook for 4 to 8 hours longer.

Keith Sutton
Alexander, AR

Sweet & Sour Canadian Goose

1 gallon cold water
1/2 cup vinegar
Skinless breast from 1 wild goose, bone-in
3 T. vegetable oil
1 T. lemon pepper, plus additional for final seasoning
1/2 cup lemon juice
1 cup honey

Combine cold water and vinegar in large non-aluminum crock or pan. Add goose breast. Cover and refrigerate overnight. (If you have done this before the goose was frozen, skip this step.)

When ready to cook, drain goose breast and pat dry; discard vinegar water. Remove bottom grate from pressure cooker, and heat oil to sizzling over medium heat. Add goose breast and lemon pepper; cook until goose is lightly browned. Transfer goose to plate. Place grate back into pressure cooker. Add lemon juice and enough water to level with the grate. Place goose back into pressure cooker, bone-side down. Pour honey over goose, and sprinkle with additional lemon pepper. Put lid on pressure cooker, seal and bring to 10 pounds pressure. Cook for **25** minutes; reduce heat as directed by manufacturer. To serve, slice breast thinly and spoon some of the cooking broth over the meat.

Variations: Substitute orange juice or pineapple juice for the lemon juice, and use brown sugar instead of honey. You may also pour some A-1 steak sauce over the meat before cooking.

Sandra L. Sullivan
Highland Springs, VA

Duck Chili with Roasted Tomatoes

<u>Advance preparation:</u>
4 wild ducks, or equivalent in pieces
3 large onions, cut into ½-inch-thick slices
6 tomatoes, halved

Roast or pressure-cook ducks. Cool ducks; remove meat and cut into bite-sized chunks, discarding bones. Prepare smoker or covered grill. Place onion slices and tomato halves onto racks that have been lightly sprayed with non-stick spray. Toss some wood chips on the fire and smoke vegetables for 45 minutes. Ducks and vegetables may be prepared 1 or 2 days in advance; refrigerate until ready to cook chili.

1 lb. ground pork
2 T. chopped garlic
Salt and pepper
1 cup flour
1 T. ground cumin
1 T. chili powder
1 cup beef or chicken broth
1 (12-oz.) can tomato sauce
1 (15-oz.) can chili beans, *optional*
1 cup chopped fresh parsley
Shredded Monterey Jack cheese
Sour cream

In medium saucepot, brown pork over medium heat, stirring to break up. Stir in garlic, and salt and pepper to taste. Add smoked tomatoes, and onions, and flour, cumin and chili powder; mix well. Add duck meat, broth, tomato sauce and beans. Mix well and simmer for 45 minutes. Stir in parsley and check seasoning; add additional chili powder if desired (for really spicy chili, also add up to a tablespoon ground cayenne pepper). Garnish with shredded cheese and sour cream.

Michael Gordon
Venice, FL

Dave's Goose Filets & Rice

Dave's Goose Filets & Rice

½ lb. long grain and wild rice mixture
Boneless, skinless breast halves from 4 wild
   geese, cut into halves (8 pieces total)
¼ cup olive oil
4 ribs celery, diced
2 small white onions, diced
2 cups sliced mushrooms
4 T. butter (half of a stick)
1 (6-oz.) can pimientos
½ cup chopped fresh dill
¼ cup chopped fresh parsley

¼ cup white zinfandel wine
2 tsp. lemon juice
2 tsp. white pepper
2 tsp. lemon pepper
2 tsp. Lawry's seasoned salt
¼ tsp. paprika
2 cups half-and-half
2 cups milk
¼ cup cornstarch, blended with
   ½ cup cold water

Prepare rice according to package directions. Spread cooked rice in 13×9×2-inch baking dish. In large skillet, brown goose breast filets well in oil over medium-high heat. Arrange browned goose breast filets over rice; set aside.

In another large skillet, sauté celery, onions and mushrooms in butter over medium heat until just tender. Add pimientos, dill and parsley, and cook for about 5 minutes longer. Add wine, lemon juice, white pepper, lemon pepper, seasoned salt and paprika. Cook for about 5 minutes longer. Transfer mixture to large saucepan. Add half-and-half and milk, and heat almost to boiling. Stirring constantly, add cornstarch slurry, a little at a time, and cook until mixture is the consistency of gravy; you may not need all of the cornstarch slurry. Pour the sauce over the filets, spreading to cover evenly. Cover dish with foil. Bake at 325°F for 2 hours, or until meat temperature is 140°F.

My family isn't real big on eating duck and goose. I keep cooking it different ways and use them as guinea pigs … I have a lot of fun and they're good sports about it. The only way they will eat my duck and goose anymore is with this recipe. I got nothing but good reports from the family last year at Christmas. Seventeen people came for dinner, and I cooked up 4 geese and 6 ducks using this recipe.

David Fry
Apple Valley, CA

Easy Italian Goose

Skinless breasts from 2 wild geese
1 (28-oz.) jar spaghetti sauce, any variety
1 cup water
Salt and pepper
Garlic salt
Seasoned salt

Place goose breasts in slow cooker. Pour spaghetti sauce and water over goose breast. Sprinkle with a few shakes each of salt, pepper, garlic salt and seasoned salt. Cover and cook on low for 10 to 12 hours.

Wynn Duell
Roulette, PA

Asian Duck Skewers

1 (14-oz.) can pineapple chunks packed in juice
2 T. teriyaki sauce
1 T. ketchup
2 tsp. cornstarch
½ tsp. chopped garlic
Boneless, skinless breast halves from 1 or 2
    wild ducks, cut into 1-inch pieces
1 red bell pepper, cut into 1-inch pieces
Half of a red onion, cut into 1-inch pieces

Drain pineapple juice into glass mixing bowl; reserve pineapple. Stir in teriyaki sauce, ketchup, cornstarch and garlic. Add duck pieces. Cover and refrigerate 1 to 4 hours, stirring occasionally.

Drain duck, reserving marinade. Alternately thread duck, pineapple, pepper and onion on skewers. In saucepan, heat marinade to boiling; brush on skewers. Grill over medium coals, turning and basting frequently, until duck is medium-rare.

Teresa Marrone
Minneapolis, MN

Duck Julius

2 or 3 wood ducks, quartered
⅓ cup Crisco oil
4 cups chopped onion
1 large bell pepper, chopped
4 cloves garlic, mashed
Cold water
Hot cooked white rice

In Dutch oven or iron pot, brown ducks in oil over medium heat until reddish brown; do not burn. Add onions, pepper and garlic. Cook, stirring frequently, until onions are transparent and reddish in color. Add enough water to cover duck. Simmer for 2½ to 3 hours, until ducks are tender; you may need to add more water if it cooks away. When ducks are tender, carefully remove and set aside until cool enough to handle. Remove meat from bones, discarding bones. Return meat back to Dutch oven and heat through. Serve duck and gravy over rice.

Mary Greider
Katy, TX

Steve's Goose & Macaroni Casserole

1 cup original-flavor Allegro marinade
½ cup red wine
2 lbs. uncooked wild goose meat, cut into 1-inch chunks
2 T. butter
1 large onion, diced
2 tsp. minced garlic

1 (16-oz.) jar "Double Cheddar" cheese pasta sauce
1 (14½-oz.) can diced tomatoes with roasted garlic
1 (10¾-oz.) can condensed tomato soup
2 (4-oz.) cans mushroom pieces
2 tsp. Monterey steak seasoning
1 (16-oz.) box elbow macaroni

In mixing bowl, combine marinade and red wine. Add goose meat; cover and refrigerate for about 12 hours. When ready to cook, melt butter in 4-quart pot. Add onion and garlic and cook over high heat until onions are almost translucent. Add goose meat and cook, stirring occasionally, until meat is browned on the outside. Add remaining ingredients except macaroni. Reduce heat to medium and cook for about 30 minutes, stirring frequently. While goose is cooking, cook macaroni according to package directions. When goose and macaroni are both done, add noodles to sauce and mix thoroughly.

Steve Gingras
Lowell, MA

Duck, Squirrel or Dove Gumbo

Flour
Salt and pepper
5 wild ducks, or 6 to 8 squirrels, or 30 doves
Shortening
1 lb. smoked sausage, cut into pieces
4 large onions, diced
8 green onions, diced
1 dried hot red chili pepper

1 clove garlic
2 springs fresh thyme
2 tsp. minced fresh parsley
1 gallon water
2 bay leaves
1 pint oysters
Hot cooked rice

Combine flour (enough for dredging meat) with salt and pepper to taste. Dredge meat in seasoned flour, then brown well in shortening in large skillet. Transfer browned meat to large dish. Brown sausage in skillet, and transfer to dish with game meat. Sauté both types of onions, red pepper, garlic, thyme and parsley in skillet, adding additional shortening if necessary, until vegetables are tender.

In large pot, melt ¼ cup shortening over medium heat. Stir in ¼ cup flour and cook, stirring constantly, until smooth and rich golden brown. Add water, stirring constantly to avoid lumps. Add bay leaves, browned meats, and vegetables; salt and pepper generously. Reduce heat and simmer for 1¾ hours. Add oysters; cook for 15 minutes longer. If desired, remove game meat from pot before adding oysters and pull meat from bones, returning meat to pot and discarding bones. Serve gumbo over rice.

Scott Adams
Meridian, TX

Hudson Valley Duck Pot Stickers

2 lbs. boneless wild duck breast meat
1 lb. boneless duck leg meat
1½ cups napa cabbage
2 T. chopped fresh gingerroot
2 T. chopped green onions
2 T. chopped fresh cilantro
2 T. sesame oil

1 T. chili oil
1 T. chopped garlic
2½ tsp. salt
1 tsp. white pepper
Wonton wrappers
Vegetable oil
One or both sauces, below

In food processor, chop all ingredients except wonton wrappers, vegetable oil and sauce. Place a teaspoon of duck filling on a wonton wrapper; fold and seal. Repeat until all duck filling is used up. Steam bundles for 5 minutes. Finish by searing in a hot skillet lightly coated with oil. Serve with sauce(s).

Oriental Sauce for Pot Stickers

1¼ cups cold water
1 cup soy sauce
1 cup mirin or sweet sake (Japanese wine)
½ cup rice vinegar
¼ cup brown sugar

1 T. chopped garlic
1 T. chopped fresh gingerroot
Arrowroot or cornstarch blended with cold
  water

In nonaluminum saucepan, combine all ingredients except arrowroot. Heat to boiling, stirring to dissolve brown sugar; reduce heat and simmer for 15 minutes, stirring occasionally. Add a small amount of the arrowroot slurry and cook until slightly thickened.

Ginger Buerre Blanc Sauce

2 cups dry sherry
½ cup chopped fresh gingerroot
¼ cup chopped shallots
2 T. sherry wine vinegar

1 cup cream
1 lb. cold unsalted butter, cut into
  small pieces
Salt

In heavy nonaluminum saucepan, combine sherry, gingerroot, shallots and vinegar. Heat to boiling over high heat, and cook until reduced to about 1 cup. Add cream and continue cooking until reduced by half. With pan over low heat, briskly whisk in small pieces of butter; allow each portion to melt and sauce to become hot again before adding additional butter pieces. Add salt to taste. Keep sauce warm over low heat to prevent sauce from separating.

Brent E. Wertz
Executive Chef, Mohonk Mountain House; New Paltz, NY

Goose Burgers

5 lbs. boneless wild goose meat
1 cup crushed soda crackers or breadcrumbs
1 medium onion, finely chopped
2 eggs, beaten
1 T. dried parsley flakes
Split hamburger rolls
Condiments: ketchup, barbecue sauce, pickles,
    sliced onions etc.

Grind goose meat through ⅛- or 3/16-inch grinder plate. In large bowl, combine ground goose with crushed crackers, onion, eggs and parsley flakes. Form into patties, and pan-fry in enough oil to prevent sticking. Serve with hamburger rolls and condiments.

This mixture can also be formed into a meat loaf, and baked in the usual way. Different from the usual meatloaf, and very good.

Aden D. Miller
Windsor, OH

Maple Duck

2- to 3-lb. wild duck
Vegetable oil
1 cup diced onion
1 cup diced celery
Fresh mushrooms, *optional*
1½ cups sauterne wine
½ cup maple syrup
2 T. grated orange rind
Hot cooked wild rice

Cut duck into small pieces and brown in a little oil in skillet. Transfer duck pieces to Dutch oven. Add remaining ingredients except wild rice to drippings in skillet, stirring to mix well and to loosen any browned bits. Pour mixture from skillet over duck pieces in Dutch oven. Bake at 300°F for 2 hours, or until duck is tender. Serve with wild rice.

David and Geraldine Smoth
Shiocton, WI

Marinated Goose

Wild goose meat
Barbecue sauce

Bone the goose, cutting meat into serving-sized pieces. Place in shallow baking dish and cover with barbecue sauce. Cover dish with foil and refrigerate for several hours, or as long as overnight. When ready to cook, bake at 250°F until meat is tender; time will vary with amount of meat.

I got this recipe from an old friend when I told him my wife didn't like wild goose because of the gamey taste. It's simple and tasty.

Jim Lord
Manchester, NH

Texas-Style Chicken-Fried Steak Duck Breasts

Boneless, skinless breast halves from
  6 wild ducks
Sprinkle-on meat tenderizer
Buttermilk
1 egg
1 T. milk

½ tsp. salt
Pepper
1 cup finely crushed saltine crackers,
  or 1 pkg. chicken fried steak coating
¼ cup vegetable oil

Sprinkle duck breasts with meat tenderizer, and pound in with meat mallet or the edge of a heavy plate. Place in nonaluminum bowl and cover with buttermilk. Cover bowl and refrigerate several hours, or as long as overnight.

When ready to cook, drain and discard buttermilk; pat duck breasts lightly dry with paper towels. In wide bowl, beat together egg, milk, salt, and pepper to taste. Place crushed saltines in another bowl. Dip duck breast filets in egg mixture, then coat with saltine crumbs. Heat oil in large skillet, and brown duck breasts on both sides, turning once. Reduce heat to low and cover skillet; cook for 30 minutes. Serve with mashed potatoes like chicken-fried steak; you won't believe it's duck.

Scott Martin
Dallas, TX

Wild Goose with Giblet Stuffing

6- to 8-lb. whole dressed wild goose
Lemon wedges
Goose giblets
2 cups water
2½ quarts crumbled cornbread
2 large Granny Smith apples, cored and chopped
1 large onion, chopped

⅓ cup minced fresh parsley
1 to 2 T. rubbed sage leaves
1 tsp. salt
¼ tsp. pepper
¼ tsp. garlic powder
Butter or margarine, softened

Rub inside of goose cavity with lemon wedges; salt generously. Set aside while you prepare the stuffing. In saucepan, cook giblets in water until tender, 20 to 30 minutes. Remove giblets with slotted spoon and reserve cooking water. Chop giblets and place in large mixing bowl. Add cornbread, apples, onion, parsley, sage, salt, pepper and garlic powder. Add enough of the reserved giblet cooking water to make a moist stuffing; toss gently. Pack body and neck cavity of goose loosely with stuffing; truss openings with small skewers, or kitchen string and a kitchen needle. Place goose, breast side up, on rack in shallow roasting pan. Spread softened butter all over goose. Bake, uncovered, at 325°F for 25 minutes per pound, or until fully cooked and tender. If goose is an older bird, add 1 cup water to pan and cover for the last hour of roasting.

Frank Bruno
Dubois, WY

**Texas-Style Chicken-Fried
Steak Duck Breasts**

Stuffed Teal with Red Wine

Whole teal or wood ducks, any quantity
1 clove garlic per 2 ducks
Salt and pepper
Marjoram
Thyme
Hot prepared bread stuffing
1 cup red wine per 2 or 3 ducks

Rub ducks with garlic; salt and pepper to taste. Place ducks in steamer without crowding and steam until legs begin to move freely; be careful not to over-steam or ducks will fall apart in next step. Remove ducks from steamer and let cool. If ducks are skin-on, gently lift skin and rub herbs between meat and skin; if ducks are skinned, rub herbs directly into meat. Stuff birds generously with prepared stuffing. Put ducks into greased baking dish, breast-side down. Pour red wine over birds. Bake at 350°F for 10 minutes. Turn ducks over and continue baking until breasts are nicely browned, being careful not to overcook.

Russ Clay
Skippack, PA

Duck, Ham & Oyster Stew

4 T. butter (half of a stick)
1 medium onion, diced
2 carrots, grated
2 cloves garlic, sliced
3 T. flour
2 cups chicken broth
2 cups beef broth
¾ cup uncooked rice
1 cup chopped cooked ham
1 bay leaf
1 tsp. crumbled dried savory leaves
1 cup chopped cooked duck meat
1 pint oysters, undrained
¼ tsp. hot red pepper flakes
Salt and cracked black pepper to taste
Buttered black bread, *optional*
Assorted olives, *optional*

In soup pot, melt butter over medium heat. Add onion, carrots and garlic and cook until tender, stirring occasionally. Whisk in flour and cook for 1 minute, stirring constantly. Whisk in chicken broth and beef broth and heat to boiling. Add rice, ham, bay leaf and savory. Reduce heat and simmer for 25 minutes, or until rice is tender. Add duck meat, oysters with their liquid, and red pepper. Simmer for 5 to 8 minutes longer. Season to taste with salt and pepper; remove bay leaf before serving. Serve with buttered black bread and a tray of assorted olives.

Andi Flanagan
Seward, AK

Jelly-Rolled Goose Breast

Boneless, skinless breast halves from
  2 wild geese
Garlic powder
Freshly ground black pepper
Salt
4 slices bacon
Barbecue sauce
Louisiana hot sauce, *optional*

Lay breast filets on cutting surface. Holding a large knife parallel to cutting surface, slice through each filet so it is half its original thickness, leaving the 2 halves attached at one end so you can open the filet up like a book. Open filets and season each side to taste with garlic powder, pepper and salt.

Lay a slice of bacon across an opened filet. Pour a line of barbecue sauce along the bacon. Roll filet up jelly-roll style, enclosing the bacon and barbecue sauce; secure with wooden toothpick. Spread additional barbecue sauce on the outside of the roll, and wrap in aluminum foil, shiny side toward the meat. Repeat until all 4 filets are rolled and wrapped. Bake at 450°F for 45 minutes, or until done to taste. Serve with Louisiana hot sauce or additional heated barbecue sauce on the side.

Keith Sutton
Alexander, AR

Easy Crock Pot Goose Breasts

Wild goose breasts
Orange juice
White wine
Chicken broth
Salt and pepper
Cornstarch blended with cold water
Wild Rice Pilaf, below

Amounts of ingredients depend on how many goose breasts you are cooking. Place goose breasts in slow cooker. Make a mixture of equal parts orange juice, white wine and chicken broth (½ cup of each is a typical amount) and pour over goose breasts. Salt and pepper to taste. Cover and cook all day. Remove goose breasts to serving platter. Thicken remaining broth with cornstarch slurry. Slice goose breasts; serve meat and gravy with wild rice pilaf.

Wild Rice Pilaf

1 lb. wild rice
2½ gallons water
1 lb. sliced bacon
2 or 3 onions, chopped
1 cup pecan halves, *optional*

Cook wild rice in water for 45 minutes, or until tender. Drain well. In large skillet, cook bacon over medium heat until crisp. Transfer cooked bacon slices to paper towel-lined plate to drain. Sauté onions in bacon drippings until tender. Crumble bacon, and combine with cooked rice, sautéed onions and pecans. This can be reheated in a 250°F oven if made in advance.

William P. Crewe
Seaford, DE

Barbequed Duck Sandwiches

1 dressed wild duck, skinned
Beer
Barbecue sauce
Sandwich rolls or hamburger buns

In saucepan, simmer duck in beer until meat is very tender. Remove duck from beer and set aside until cool enough to handle. Remove meat from bones, discarding bones. Mix meat with barbecue sauce and more beer until the sauce has thickened and reduced to a manageable amount. Serve meat on sandwich rolls or hamburger buns. Great with chips!

Shell Bleiweiss
Barrington, IL

Duck/Goose Roll-Ups

Boneless, skinless breast halves from wild
  ducks or geese
Garlic salt
Grated Parmesan cheese
Pickled jalapeño peppers

Cut duck or goose breasts into ¼- to ³⁄₈-inch strips. Pound with a meat mallet or the edge of a heavy saucer to flatten and tenderize. Sprinkle each slice with garlic salt and Parmesan cheese. Lay 2 or 3 pickled jalapeño slices on each strip of meat and roll up; secure with wooden toothpick. Grill for 10 to 15 minutes.

Steve Barber
Arlington, TX

Pintail on the Stuffing

3 cups cooked rice
3 ribs celery, chopped
1 large onion, chopped
2 cloves garlic, minced
1 cup golden raisins
1 (6-oz.) can crushed pineapple
3 eggs, lightly beaten
1 tsp. poultry seasoning
1 tsp. freshly cracked pepper
½ tsp. salt
1 stick butter (8 T.), melted, divided
4 whole dressed pintails, cut into halves
Braised red cabbage, *optional*
Baked apples, *optional*

In large mixing bowl, combine rice, celery, onion, garlic, raisins, pineapple, eggs, poultry seasoning, cracked pepper and salt. Mix well. Pour half of the melted butter over the mixture and stir again. Pack rice mixture into 13×9×2-inch baking dish. Lay ducks on top of rice, and sprinkle with a little additional salt, pepper and poultry seasoning. Cover dish tightly and bake at 400°F for one hour. Remove foil and brush ducks with some of the remaining melted butter. Continue baking for 30 minutes longer or until pintails are rich brown, basting occasionally with the melted butter. Serve with braised red cabbage and baked apples.

Andi Flanagan
Seward, AK

Pintail on the
Stuffing

Marinated Duck Breast with Gravy

Boneless breast halves from 6 to 10
   wild ducks
Bottled Italian dressing
1 or 2 packs peppered bacon
1 onion, chopped
2 tsp. vegetable oil
2 (1-oz.) pkgs. dry brown gravy mix

Cut breast pieces in half and place in non-aluminum baking dish. Pour Italian dressing over breast filets, turning to coat. Cover and refrigerate for 2 or 3 hours. Remove breast filets from dressing; discard dressing. Wrap bacon around breast filets and place in baking dish. In skillet, brown onion in oil over medium-high heat. Mix gravy as directed on package and add to onion, stirring to combine. Pour gravy mixture over ducks. Bake at 350°F for about 1 hour, or until cooked through and tender.

Reita Lofland
Horatio, AR

St. Clair Flats Duck Breast Stew

Skinless breasts from 4 to 6 mallard,
   canvasback or other large wild ducks
1 (18-oz.) bottle Heinz 57 steak sauce
6 small to medium apples, peeled and cored
1 large onion, cut into halves
2 T. cinnamon
1½ quarts uncooked wild rice
1 (1-lb.) bag fresh cranberries

Place duck breasts in slow cooker. Pour steak sauce over duck breasts. Add 4 of the apples and one onion half. Cover and cook on high for 2½ hours. Dice 2 remaining apples and remaining onion half, and stir into slow cooker. Sprinkle cinnamon over top. Re-cover and cook for 2½ hours longer. Cook wild rice in separate pot, adding cranberries. To serve, pour stew over rice-cranberry mixture.

Mike Szudarek
Warren, MI

Goose Breast Sandwiches with Peppers & Onions

Boneless, skinless breast halves from 1 wild goose
Milk
1 (1-oz.) pkg. dry beef gravy mix
Flour
1 egg, beaten

Italian breadcrumbs
1 bell pepper, sliced
1 medium onion, sliced
Vegetable oil
Sandwich buns or bread

Place goose in glass dish. Cover with milk. Cover and refrigerate for 12 hours. Remove goose from milk; discard milk. Pat goose breast dry and fillet goose breast from bone (if you started with filets, simply proceed with recipe). Sprinkle Gravy Master over goose; cover and refrigerate for 3 to 4 hours.

When ready to cook, pat goose breast filets dry. Dip in flour to coat. Dip floured filets in beaten egg, then into Italian breadcrumbs; set aside. In skillet, sauté pepper and onion in a little oil over medium heat until tender; set aside and keep warm while you fry goose breast filets.

Heat oil in deep fryer, or deep skillet. Deep-fry coated filets for 3 to 5 minutes, or until cooked through. Serve goose breast filets as a sandwich, topped with peppers and onions; these are also good as a main meal without the bread.

Bill Sciuti
Islip, NY

Berry Good Teal

¼ cup canola oil
Juice of one lemon
1½ tsp. rosemary leaves, lightly crushed
6 to 8 whole teal
1 to 2 T. brown sugar

1½ cups blueberries
½ cup lowbush cranberries, or
  chopped store-bought cranberries
6 to 8 T. butter (three-quarters to 1 stick)
A little cornstarch blended with cold water

In small saucepan, heat oil, lemon juice and rosemary over very low heat, stirring just to blend. Brush teal inside and out with this mixture; save any leftover sauce for basting. Put ½ teaspoon brown sugar in each teal cavity. Mix berries together, and stuff teal with mixed berries. Place 1 tablespoon butter in each teal cavity. Wrap teal individually in foil, sealing tightly. Place foil-wrapped teal breast side down on rack in roasting pan. Bake at 425°F for 35 minutes. Open each foil packet carefully and pour juices into a saucepan. Place unwrapped birds back on roasting rack, breast side up, and return to oven to brown, basting with the lemon mixture. Transfer browned teal to hot platter and pour any juices in the roaster into the saucepan with the other roasting juices. Thicken with cornstarch slurry; serve with teal.

Andi Flanagan
Seward, AK

SMALL GAME

Squirrel & Andouille Sausage Gumbo

2 sticks butter (½ lb.)
¼ cup flour
1 medium onion, chopped
1 green bell pepper, chopped
1 jalapeño pepper, chopped
2 ribs celery, chopped
6 cloves garlic, minced
Squirrel stock and meat from recipe below

3 bay leaves
1 T. salt
1 T. black pepper
2 tsp. crumbled dried oregano leaves
2 tsp. crumbled dried thyme leaves
2 links andouille sausage, or your favorite link sausage
Hot cooked rice

Make roux: Melt butter in large heavy-bottomed saucepan over medium-low heat. Add flour, stirring constantly, and cook until mixture reaches a dark brown color (resembling the color of milk chocolate), stirring constantly. Be very careful not to burn, especially near the end of cooking; if any black specks appear, discard the mixture and start over.

As soon as roux is chocolate-colored, add onion, peppers, celery and garlic. Cook, stirring frequently, until onions become clear. Add squirrel stock and enough water to fill pot, whisking well to incorporate. Add squirrel meat and remaining ingredients except rice. Heat to boiling. Reduce heat and simmer for 30 to 45 minutes, stirring occasionally. Serve over rice.

Squirrel Stock & Meat

4 or 5 squirrels
1 medium onion, cut into large chunks
2 ribs celery, cut into 1-inch pieces
2 carrots, peeled and cut into 1-inch pieces

1 or 2 jalapeño peppers, cut into halves
1 tsp. crumbled dried thyme leaves
3 bay leaves
10 peppercorns, crushed

Combine all ingredients in large saucepan. Cover with cold water. Heat to boiling, then reduce heat and simmer for 30 to 45 minutes, or until squirrels are cooked through. Strain into another pot through colander, reserving stock. Transfer squirrels to a plate and set aside until cool enough to handle; discard vegetables from colander. Pick squirrel meat from bones, discarding bones. Stock and squirrel meat are now ready to make gumbo, above.

Joseph Smith
Austin, TX

Squirrel & Andouille Sausage Gumbo

Timberline Stew

3 squirrels
2 onions, chopped
2 potatoes, diced
1 green bell pepper, chopped
¼ cup diced celery
½ tsp. garlic powder
Dash of hot sauce
Salt and pepper to taste
1 cup cooked rice or egg noodles

Cook squirrels by pressure-cooking, or by boiling in water to cover until tender. Remove from cooking broth; when cool enough to handle, pull meat from bones and return to broth, discarding bones. Heat to boiling. Add all ingredients except rice. Cook at a gentle boil until vegetables are tender. Add cooked rice and heat until hot.

Harold "Scottie" Scott
Cincinnati, OH

Mom's Fried Rabbit

2 rabbits, cut into pieces
1 quart salted water
1 cup wine vinegar
2 eggs, beaten
1 cup Italian-seasoned breadcrumbs
½ cup vegetable oil

In large pot, soak rabbit pieces in salted water overnight in refrigerator. The next day, add vinegar and cook at a rapid boil for 1 hour. Let cool, and refrigerate for 2 hours. Pat rabbit pieces dry with paper towels. Dip into egg, then into breadcrumbs. In large skillet, fry coated rabbit pieces in hot oil until nicely browned on both sides.

Frank Schilling
Levittown, PA

Rabbit Pie

2 young rabbits, cut into pieces
1 onion, sliced
1 slice bacon, cut into pieces
1 tsp. salt
Dash of pepper
Boiling water, approx. 1 quart
Flour for thickening
Homemade or commercial mix for rich
   biscuit dough

In large saucepan, combine rabbit, onion, bacon, salt and pepper. Add boiling water to cover. Cover and simmer until rabbit is tender. Transfer rabbit to dish to cool. Thicken broth with flour, using 2 tablespoons to each cup liquid. Remove rabbit meat from bones, discarding bones. Return rabbit meat to thickened broth and stir to combine. Pour mixture into baking dish. Prepare enough biscuit dough to cover top of baking dish when rolled out ¼ inch thick. Roll or pat biscuit dough out on floured board, and cover top of baking dish with dough. Cut slits in dough to allow steam to escape. Bake at 450°F for 30 minutes.

Chris and Wanda DeVore
Chehalis, WA

Pulled Raccoon

3 raccoons
1 bell pepper, diced
Half of a purple onion, diced
1 (10-oz.) bottle barbecue sauce
1 (12-oz.) can beer
1 T. pepper
1 T. lemon juice
Salt to taste
Toasted buns

Parboil raccoons in water to cover for 2 to 2½ hours, or until meat is easy to pull from bone. Drain raccoons and let cool. Pull meat from bones, discarding bones. Place meat and all remaining ingredients except buns in mixing bowl or large pot; mix thoroughly. Cover and refrigerate overnight, stirring 2 or 3 times.

When ready to cook, you have 2 options. My favorite is to cook the mixture on a smoker for 3 to 4 hours, stirring often; the taste is excellent. Or, you can cook in the oven at 350°F for 1 to 1½ hours, stirring often. Serve in toasted buns. Baked potato and sweet carrots are great side dishes for this meal.

Grey "Sparky" Sparkman
Gordonville, MO

5-Megaton Chili

1 small rabbit, cut into pieces
Boneless, skinless breast halves from 1 grouse
2 boneless, skinless chicken breast halves
½ lb. ground venison
½ lb. ground beef
Garlic powder to taste
2 drops Tabasco sauce
1 (14-oz.) can red kidney beans, drained
2 (10-oz.) cans mushroom stems and
  pieces, drained
1 (28-oz.) can tomato sauce
1 or 2 pouches chili mix

Simmer rabbit, grouse breast and chicken breast in water to cover until tender; if some pieces become tender before the other pieces, remove them and continue cooking other pieces until everything is cooked. Cool and remove meat from bones; cut into bite-sized pieces, discarding bones. This may be done a day in advance; place meat in covered dish and refrigerate until ready to cook.

In large pot or Dutch oven, combine venison, beef, garlic powder and Tabasco sauce. Cook until venison and beef are brown, stirring to break up. Add cut-up cooked rabbit, grouse and chicken and remaining ingredients, using 1 pouch chili mix for mild and 2 for hot. Simmer at lowest setting for an hour or longer, or until chili is done to taste.

Serve chili in a bowl with toast and a cold mug of beer. Put the Tabasco sauce on the table for the more suicidal.

George Sanders
Sudbury, ONT

Baked Squirrel

2 squirrels, cut into pieces
4 medium potatoes, quartered
1 large onion, sliced
2 cups water
¼ cup breadcrumbs
¼ cup flour
1 tsp. Italian seasoning
1 tsp. garlic powder
½ tsp. ground coriander
½ tsp. paprika
1 stick butter (8 T.), cut into pieces

Combine squirrel and potatoes in casserole dish; top with onion slices. Pour water over onion slices. In small bowl, mix together breadcrumbs, flour, Italian seasoning, garlic powder, coriander and paprika. Sprinkle over onion slices. Scatter butter over the top. Cover and bake at 375°F until meat flakes easily from bones. Uncover and bake for 10 minutes longer.

Aden D. Miller
Windsor, OH

Peachy Coon

Raccoon hindquarters
Garlic powder
Salt and pepper
1 (29-oz.) can peaches, drained
1 cup honey
½ cup red wine

Arrange racoon in baking pan or roaster. Season to taste with garlic powder, salt and pepper. Combine peaches, honey and wine in blender, and process until smooth. Brush half of peach glaze over meat. Cover and bake at 400°F, brushing frequently with remaining glaze, until meat is tender and done, 1 to 1½ hours.

M.L. Allen
Vermillion, SD

Baked Snowshoe

1 hare, cut into 8 pieces
2 cups red wine, port or claret
2 large onions, sliced
1 T. mixed pickling spices
1 tsp. salt
⅛ tsp. pepper
1 stick butter or margarine (8 T.)
1 herb bouquet (parsley, thyme, bay leaf)
2 cups hot bouillon or beef broth
Instantized flour, such as Wondra

In large bowl, combine hare, wine, onions, spices, salt and pepper. Cover and refrigerate for 1 or 2 days, turning hare occasionally. When ready to cook, remove hare and pat dry; reserve marinade. In heatproof casserole, melt butter; brown hare on all sides. Remove from heat; add marinade and herb bouquet. Cover and bake at 350°F for 2 to 3 hours. During last half hour of baking, sprinkle with flour and stir. Continue baking, uncovered, for remaining time. Thicken gravy with more flour; strain and pour over hare.

Clete Bellin
Forestville, WI

Big Joe's Wild Game & Corn Chowder

1 cup uncooked boneless wild rabbit or
    squirrel meat, cut into small pieces
1 T. butter
2 baked potatoes, skinned
2 cans sweet corn, undrained
1 (10¾-oz.) can cream of mushroom soup
⅓ cup milk
1 T. grated Parmesan cheese

1 T. Old Bay seasoning
⅛ tsp. garlic salt
5 dashes Texas Pete or other spicy seasoning
Pinch of ground cayenne pepper
Pinch of black pepper
Sour cream for garnish
Fresh parsley for garnish

In large pot, fry rabbit in butter just until cooked through. Drain and discard excess grease if necessary. Mash potatoes and add to pot with rabbit. Add all remaining ingredients except sour cream and parsley; stir well. Heat just to boiling; reduce heat and simmer for 5 minutes, stirring occasionally. Garnish individual servings with sour cream and parsley.

Joe Davis
Shipman, VA

Rabbit Sauce Piquante

2 wild rabbits, cut into serving pieces
Salt and pepper to taste
½ tsp. ground cayenne pepper
1 cup plus 2 T. vegetable oil, divided
½ cup water
¼ cup flour
1 cup chopped onion
1 cup chopped celery

½ cup minced green bell peppers
1 cup dry white wine, or water
1 (6-oz). can tomato paste
2 T. browning sauce such as Kitchen Bouquet
3 cloves garlic, minced
½ cup minced green onion tops
¼ cup minced fresh parsley
2 to 3 cups hot cooked rice

Season rabbits with salt, pepper and cayenne. In large skillet, heat 1 cup of the oil and pan-fry rabbit for 8 minutes, turning frequently. Add water; cover tightly and simmer for about 25 minutes.

Meanwhile, in Dutch oven, cook flour in remaining 2 tablespoons oil over medium heat, stirring constantly, until mixture is a rich golden brown. Add onion, celery and bell peppers; cook until vegetables are wilted, stirring occasionally. Add wine, tomato paste and browning sauce to Dutch oven. Cook until vegetables are desired doneness, stirring occasionally.

When rabbit has simmered for about 25 minutes, transfer rabbit pieces to Dutch oven with vegetables. Add garlic and cook for 20 minutes, stirring occasionally. Add onion tops and parsley; cook for 10 minutes longer. Serve rabbit and sauce over rice.

Dana Parker
Vancleave, MS

Rabbit Bake
with Herb
Dumplings

Rabbit Bake with Herb Dumplings

1/3 cup flour
1 tsp. paprika
1/2 tsp. salt
1/8 tsp. pepper
1 wild rabbit, cut into pieces
Vegetable shortening
1/4 cup water
1 large onion, chopped coarsely
1 (10 3/4-oz.) can cream of mushroom soup

Herb dumplings:
1/2 cup dry breadcrumbs
1 T. poppy seed
1 tsp. poultry seasoning
1 tsp. celery seed
1 tsp. dried onion flakes
1 tube refrigerated buttermilk biscuits
Melted butter

In shallow dish, mix flour, paprika, salt and pepper. Dredge rabbit in flour mixture. Melt shortening in skillet; brown rabbit pieces on all sides, turning frequently. Add water to skillet. Cover and simmer until rabbit is tender, 1 to 1½ hours. Uncover skillet; set rabbit pieces aside until cool enough to handle.

Cut rabbit meat from bones in large pieces, discarding bones. Place rabbit and onion in 2-quart casserole. Add soup to drippings in skillet and stir well. Pour soup over rabbit.

To make the dumplings, combine breadcrumbs, poppy seed, poultry seasoning, celery seed and onion flakes in wide bowl. Dip biscuits into melted butter, then into crumb mixture. Arrange biscuits around edge of casserole. Bake at 400°F for 20 to 25 minutes, until deep golden brown.

Doralee Zeneberg
Traverse City, MI

Pan-Fried Muskrat with Sweet Milk Gravy

1 muskrat, cut into serving pieces
Salt and freshly ground black pepper
1 egg
1½ cups milk, divided

Flour
Cracker meal
3 T. bacon drippings

Parboil muskrat pieces in water to cover until tender. Remove, pat dry with paper towels, and season with salt and pepper. In mixing bowl, beat together egg and about a tablespoon of the milk. Dredge muskrat pieces in flour, then dip in egg mixture. Coat with cracker meal. Heat bacon drippings in large skillet. Add coated muskrat pieces, reduce heat to low, and cook until browned on both sides. Transfer browned muskrat to warmed serving platter; cover loosely and set aside.

To make gravy, scrape bottom of skillet to loosen cracklings. Stir 3 tablespoons flour into skillet and cook over medium heat for a minute or two, stirring constantly. Pour remaining milk (not quite 1½ cups) into skillet and cook, stirring constantly, until gravy thickens and bubbles. Serve gravy over muskrat.

Keith Sutton
Alexander, AR

Greek Rabbit

10 potatoes, quartered
2 or 3 wild rabbits, cut into serving pieces
1 cup olive oil
½ cup lemon juice
1 T. instant minced onion
1 tsp. crumbled dried oregano leaves
½ tsp. lemon pepper
¼ tsp. minced garlic

Parboil potatoes for 10 minutes in water to cover; drain well. Arrange rabbit pieces in large baking dish. Distribute potatoes evenly over rabbit pieces. In mixing bowl, combine remaining ingredients and blend together with fork or whisk. Pour oil mixture over rabbits and potatoes. Bake at 350°F for 1 hour.

Craig Bohbrink
Brownsburg, IN

Hog-Tied Rabbit

2 or 3 wild rabbits, cut into 10 to 15 pieces
1 (16-oz.) pkg. sliced bacon
1 pkg. pork-flavor Shake 'n Bake mix
½ tsp. lemon pepper
½ tsp. onion salt

Parboil rabbit pieces in water to cover for 15 minutes. Drain pieces and pat dry; set aside until cool. Cut several slits into each piece. Wrap each piece with a strip of bacon; secure with wooden toothpicks. In shaker bag provided with baking mix, combine baking mix with lemon pepper and onion salt; shake well to mix. Add rabbit pieces and shake gently to coat. Arrange pieces in single layer on baking sheet. Bake at 350°F for 45 minutes, or until brown and crispy.

John S. Watson
Freedom, PA

Sherry-Baked Rabbit

1 wild rabbit, cut into pieces
Flour seasoned with salt and pepper
6 T. butter (three-quarters of a stick), divided
1 medium onion, chopped
1 cup ketchup
½ cup sherry
⅓ cup water
2 T. lemon juice
1 T. Worcestershire sauce
1 T. brown sugar

Dredge rabbit in seasoned flour. Melt ¼ cup of the butter in skillet over medium heat, and brown rabbit on all sides. Transfer rabbit to 2-quart casserole. Combine remaining 2 tablespoons butter and all remaining ingredients in saucepan; heat to boiling. Pour over rabbit. Bake at 325°F for 1 hour, or until tender.

Arthur Van Dommelen
De Pere, WI

Bourbon Rabbit

Marinade:
½ cup olive oil
½ cup bourbon whiskey
½ cup red wine
¼ cup molasses
1 tsp. crumbled dried thyme leaves
1 tsp. crumbled dried rosemary leaves

2 or 3 large wild rabbits, or 3 or 4 small
   wild rabbits, cut into small pieces
¼ lb. thick-sliced bacon, cut into small pieces
1 lb. sliced mushrooms
4 medium carrots, sliced
1 large onion, chopped
¼ cup chopped celery
1 cup bourbon
1 cup red wine
1 to 1½ cups chicken broth
Hot cooked rice or mashed potatoes

In large bowl, combine all marinade ingredients. Add rabbit pieces. Cover and refrigerate at least 8 hours, or as long as overnight.

When ready to cook, fry bacon in large oven-proof skillet over medium heat until lightly browned. With slotted spoon, transfer bacon to dish; set aside. Drain rabbit and pat dry; discard marinade. Sauté rabbit pieces in bacon drippings until meat changes color; transfer to dish with bacon. Add mushrooms, carrots, onion and celery to skillet. Sauté until onions are tender, stirring occasionally. Add bourbon and red wine to skillet. Cook over high heat until liquid is reduced to half original volume. Add chicken stock to skillet and stir well. Return rabbit and bacon to skillet. Bake at 325°F for 45 minutes. Serve over rice or mashed potatoes.

Linda Fields
Booneville, KY

Rabbit à la King

1 T. vegetable oil
Boneless meat from 2 wild rabbits, cut into
   bite-sized pieces
1 carrot, thinly sliced
Dash of pepper
Dash of salt
Dash of garlic powder
¼ cup margarine (half of a stick)
¼ cup flour
1½ cups milk
1 cup frozen peas
2 slices Swiss cheese
2 heaping T. sour cream
Hot cooked rice, biscuits or noodles

In large skillet, heat oil over medium heat. Add rabbit and carrot. Sprinkle with pepper, salt and garlic powder and cook until rabbit is cooked through, stirring occasionally. Transfer rabbit and carrots to dish; set aside.

Add margarine to same skillet and melt over medium heat. Sprinkle flour into skillet and cook, stirring constantly, until mixture is smooth and bubbly. Stir in milk and cook, stirring constantly, until sauce thickens and bubbles. Return rabbit and carrots to skillet. Add peas, Swiss cheese and sour cream. Simmer for 5 to 10 minutes, stirring occasionally; make sure that cheese melts and peas are warmed through. Serve over rice, biscuits or noodles.

Michael Fair
Orange Park, FL

Black-and-Tan Rabbit Stew

4 slices bacon, diced
1 lb. boneless uncooked wild rabbit meat,
　　cut into 1-inch pieces
1 medium onion, coarsely chopped
2 cloves garlic, minced
1 cup stout, such as Guinness
1 (12-oz.) bottle ale, such as Bass or Harp

3 T. instant mashed potato flakes
1 tsp. Dijon-style mustard
½ tsp. crumbled dried marjoram leaves
½ tsp. salt
1 cup baby carrots
Additional stout and ale for
　　Black and Tans if desired

Cook bacon over low heat in heavy nonaluminum skillet until crisp and brown. Use slotted spoon to transfer bacon to small Dutch oven or casserole dish; set aside. Add half of the rabbit pieces to skillet with bacon drippings and brown on all sides. Use slotted spoon to transfer rabbit meat to Dutch oven with bacon; repeat with remaining rabbit meat, transferring to Dutch oven when browned. Add onions and garlic to skillet and cook until lightly browned, stirring frequently. Transfer to Dutch oven. Add stout to skillet, stirring to loosen browned bits. Cook over high heat until liquid has reduced to a syrupy glaze. Stir in ale, potato flakes, mustard, marjoram and salt; heat to boiling and cook about 1 minute. Add ale mixture and carrots to Dutch oven, and stir gently to combine all ingredients. Cover Dutch oven and bake at 325°F for 1½ hours.

This dish gets its name—and flavor—from stout and ale, which combine to make the famous British beverage Black and Tan. For a wonderful meal, serve Black and Tans with the stew (recipe below), along with some crusty bread and sweet butter.

Black-and-Tans

Ale, such as Bass or Harp
Stout, such as Guinness

Fill a pint glass ⅔ full with ale, then hold a spoon in place so the bowl of the spoon rests on the top surface of the ale. Slowly and carefully pour stout into the spoon, raising the spoon as the glass is filled so the stout is not poured directly into the ale. This should yield the classic two-layered Black and Tan, with the ale on the bottom and a layer of dark stout on top.

Teresa Marrone
Minneapolis, MN

Black-and-Tan
Rabbit Stew

Squirrel Pot Pie

6 to 8 squirrels
2 cups flour
1 egg
½ cup milk
Dash of salt
Dash of pepper
6 to 8 potatoes, peeled and diced
½ cup diced onion

In large pot, cook squirrels by boiling in water to cover until tender. Remove from cooking broth, reserving broth; when squirrels are cool enough to handle, pull meat from bones, discarding bones.

In mixing bowl, combine flour, egg, milk, salt and pepper. Work into a small ball. On lightly floured board, roll dough ⅛ inch thick. Cut into 3-inch squares.

Heat reserved broth to boiling. Drop dough squares, squirrel meat, potatoes and onion into boiling broth, adding in layers until everything is in the pot. Cover pot and cook for 20 to 30 minutes, or until potatoes are tender and dough squares are cooked.

Grace Noll
Mifflinburg, PA

Rabbit on a Ritz

1½ cups chopped cooked rabbit meat
¼ cup chopped celery
¼ cup chopped onion
2 T. diced pimiento
¼ tsp. salt
¼ tsp. black pepper
¼ tsp. ground red pepper, *optional*
½ cup ranch salad dressing
1 box Ritz crackers

In mixing bowl, combine rabbit, celery, onion, pimiento, salt, black pepper and red pepper; mix well. Add salad dressing and stir until well blended. Cover and chill for several hours before serving. Serve with Ritz crackers. This goes great with an after-dinner wine.

Gary L. Hauser
Akron, OH

Ground Coon Steaks

1 lb. ground raccoon (see notes below)
½ cup breadcrumbs
¼ cup heavy cream
1 egg, beaten
1 medium onion, finely chopped
2 cloves garlic, minced
Salt and pepper
1 quart beef broth
Cornstarch mixed with cold water
Hot cooked rice

Combine raccoon, breadcrumbs, cream, egg, onion, garlic, and salt and pepper to taste; mix well. Form into thick patties. In large skillet, heat beef broth to simmering. Place patties in simmering broth. Cover and let simmer until patties are tender and cooked through; do not allow broth to boil. Transfer cooked patties to serving dish. Thicken broth with cornstarch slurry. Serve patties and sauce over rice.

Notes on making ground raccoon: We usually use older, tougher racoon for grinding. The color of the meat tells you a lot about the racoon's age. Our motto at home is, the pinker the better, since pink denotes a young racoon. If the meat is purple, grind it; but if it's maroon, boil it for dog food. We *never* give our hounds raw racoon.

Single grinding will produce tough meat, so we grind the meat twice through the same grinding plate for a more tender finished product. A grinding plate with large holes helps prevent the tendons from clogging the grinder.

You control the amount of fat in the ground coon. There is usually plenty of fat layered between the muscles, especially on the hindquarters. If you prefer more, add a little fatty bacon. The best way to test for fat is to fry a small amount in a skillet.

M.L. Allen
Vermillion, SD

Too Much Shot Stew

2 wild rabbits, or equivalent of other
    small game
1¼ quarts water
1 chicken bouillon cube
3 or 4 medium potatoes, diced
1 medium onion, diced
1 to 2 cups frozen corn kernels
1 to 2 cups frozen beans
1 to 2 cups frozen peas
1 small bag baby carrots, or 1 cup shredded
Salt and pepper
Oyster crackers

In Dutch oven, combine rabbits, water and bouillon cube. Heat to boiling and cook until meat is falling from the bones. Transfer rabbits to dish, reserving broth; when cool enough to handle, remove meat from bones, squeezing out any shot pellets in the meat. If there are small bone particles or shot in the broth, strain broth through doubled cheesecloth.

Return meat to broth. Add remaining ingredients except salt, pepper and oyster crackers. Cover and cook on low for 30 to 40 minutes; salt and pepper to taste. Serve with oyster crackers.

This recipe is for you folks that shoot game with too much gun! It's a great way to use the meat from a shot-up rabbit, squirrel or whatever.

Steve Edsall
De Witt, MI

Squirrels in Cream

2 small squirrels, cut into pieces
Salted water
½ cup diced ham
1 onion, finely chopped
1 (4-oz.) can sliced mushrooms, drained
1 cup beef bouillon
½ tsp. crumbled dried thyme leaves
1 cup sour cream
3 T. flour
2 T. lemon juice
Minced parsley for garnish

Marinate squirrel overnight in salted water in refrigerator. When ready to cook, drain squirrel pieces and pat dry. Place squirrel, ham, onion, mushrooms, bouillon and thyme in slow cooker. Cover and cook on low for 8 to 10 hours. Before serving, turn slow cooker to high. Transfer squirrel to heated platter; set aside. In small bowl, combine sour cream, flour and lemon juice. Stir sour cream mixture into juices in slow cooker. Cook until thickened. Spoon sauce over squirrel and sprinkle with parsley.

Michael Fair
Orange Park, FL

Craig's BBQ Raccoon

1 small to medium raccoon
1 T. butter
1 tsp. minced garlic
½ cup ketchup
⅓ cup chili sauce
2 T. brown sugar
2 T. chopped onion
1 T. Worcestershire sauce
1 T. prepared mustard
Dash of Tabasco sauce
Dash of lemon juice
Salt to taste

In large pot, parboil raccoon in water to cover for 45 minutes. Drain, discarding water; cut raccoon into pieces. Transfer to slow cooker.

In saucepan, melt butter over medium heat. Add garlic and cook for 4 to 5 minutes, stirring occasionally. Add remaining ingredients. Heat to boiling. Pour sauce over raccoon in slow cooker. Cover and cook on high for 3 hours.

Note: Double sauce ingredients for large raccoon, or more than one smaller raccoon.

Craig Bohbrink
Brownsburg, IN

Cream of Brie & Rabbit Soup

Boneless meat from 1 wild rabbit, cubed
½ cup diced Vidalia or other onion
½ cup thinly sliced celery
4 T. butter (half of a stick)
¼ cup flour
2 cups milk

2 cups chicken broth
¾ lb. brie cheese, cubed
¼ lb. cheddar cheese, shredded or cubed
Salt and pepper
Fresh snipped chives for garnish

In soup pot or Dutch oven, sauté rabbit, onion and celery in butter until rabbit is medium rare and vegetables are limp. Remove rabbit meat from pot; set aside. Stir flour into pot with vegetables. Remove from heat; add milk and broth, whisking well to blend. Return pot to heat and cook, stirring constantly, until soup thickens somewhat. Add brie and cheddar cheeses and cook, stirring constantly, until cheeses melt. Pour soup into food processor and process until smooth. Return soup to pot and add rabbit; heat over low heat for a moment to re-heat rabbit. Stir in salt and pepper to taste. Garnish with chives.

This soup has been devoured by many friends who swore they would never eat rabbit or any wild animal! It is a very smooth and cheesy soup that could be prepared in many variations, such as adding ham or bacon or whatever you like.

Mike Collins
Howell, MI

T.J. & M.J.'s Rabbit Filets

2 eggs
3 T. minced fresh parsley, divided
Salt and pepper
2 cups breadcrumbs
¾ cup grated Romano cheese

½ tsp. paprika
1½ to 2 lbs. boneless rabbit filets
2 T. vegetable oil
¼ to ½ cup water

Beat together eggs, 1 tablespoon of the parsley, and salt and pepper to taste. In another dish, combine breadcrumbs, Romano cheese, 1 teaspoon salt, ½ teaspoon pepper and the paprika; mix well. Dip rabbit filets in egg mixture, then into crumb mixture, coating both sides. Heat oil in skillet. Add rabbit filets and brown for 3 to 4 minutes on each side. Transfer browned filets to baking dish or casserole in single layer; add water around filets. Cover dish with foil. Bake at 350°F for about 1½ hours, or until tender.

Note: You may also drizzle a small amount of butter, melted with garlic or your favorite seasoning, over the filets just prior to baking. For convenience, filets can be breaded and refrigerated as much as a day ahead; you may also bread, brown, cool and freeze the filets for baking at another time. We have used this recipe for our wild game dinners since 1987. This recipe is also good with deer filets.

Thomas J. Madeline
Fountain Inn, SC

BBQ Beaver-Wiches

BBQ Beaver-Wiches

1 medium beaver, cut into serving pieces
1 cup chili sauce
1 cup beer
3 T. brown sugar
2 T. minced onion
1 T. minced garlic
2 tsp. Worcestershire sauce
1 tsp. dry mustard
½ tsp. liquid smoke
Dash hot pepper sauce
Salt and black pepper to taste
Kaiser rolls
Cole slaw for a relish

In Dutch oven, combine all ingredients except Kaiser rolls and cole slaw; stir well to mix. Heat to boiling. Reduce heat and simmer for 1½ hours, or until meat is falling from bone. Remove beaver pieces with tongs and set aside until cool enough to handle. Pull meat from bones and return to sauce; discard bones. Reheat gently if necessary. Warm Kaiser rolls in oven and fill with meat mixture. Top with cole slaw. This is also very good served over rice.

Andi Flanagan
Seward, AK

Shake-n-Bake Squirrel

2 to 4 squirrels
1 pkg. barbecue-flavor Shake 'n Bake mix

Cut squirrels into 5 pieces each: 2 front legs, 2 back legs, and back. If squirrels are large or old, cover with water in saucepan and heat to boiling; boil 10 to 15 minutes, then drain well. If squirrels are young, boiling is not necessary; simply rinse young squirrel pieces in cold water.

Place moist squirrel pieces in shaker bag from baking mix. Add mix and shake to coat. Arrange pieces in single layer on baking sheet. Bake at 425°F for 30 to 35 minutes, or until crispy. The squirrel will be very tender and tasty.

Justin Claar
Bedford, PA

Jackrabbit Stew

1 jackrabbit, boned and cubed
1 to 2 quarts water
4 potatoes, cubed
4 carrots, cubed
3 T. flour
1 tsp. salt
1 tsp. pepper
1 tsp. browning sauce such as Kitchen
   Bouquet
Fresh-baked bread, *optional*

In 4-quart pan, combine rabbit and water to cover by an inch. Boil until meat is tender. Add potatoes and carrots, and continue cooking until vegetables are tender. Stir in flour and cook until sauce thickens and bubbles. Add salt, pepper and browning sauce. Serve with bread.

John A. Voaklander
Osage, IA

JERKY,
SAUSAGE &
SMOKEHOUSE

Moose Hot Sausage

8 lbs. ground moose
2 lbs. ground pork
6 T. paprika
3 T. plus 1½ tsp. garlic powder
2 T. fennel seed
1 T. plus 2 tsp. hot red pepper flakes
1 T. black pepper
1 T. ground sage
2 tsp. onion salt

In large bowl, combine all ingredients and mix very well. Test for seasoning by frying a small patty; correct seasoning if necessary. Shape sausage into patties. Layer patties with waxed paper for freezing. To cook, pan-fry or bake until cooked through.

Paul J. Woychik
Arcadia, WI

Coon Sausage

1 lb. ground raccoon (see page 129)
1¼ tsp. ground sage
1 tsp. crumbled dried thyme leaves
½ tsp. garlic powder
½ tsp. crumbled dried savory leaves
¼ tsp. crumbled dried marjoram leaves
¼ tsp. black pepper
¼ tsp. salt
⅛ tsp. ground cloves
Ground cayenne pepper to taste, *optional*

In large bowl, combine all ingredients and mix very well. Test for seasoning by frying a small patty; correct seasoning if necessary. Try this sausage in your biscuits-and-gravy recipe!

M.L. Allen
Vermillion, SD

Mike's Smoked Bird

2 cups Morton Tender Quick curing salt
1 cup canning/pickling salt
½ cup liquid smoke
1½ to 2 gal. cold water
10- to 12-lb. wild turkey, or any other game-bird such as goose, duck etc.

In clean 5-gallon plastic pail or other large nonaluminum container, combine curing salt, canning salt, liquid smoke and cold water; stir until salt dissolves completely. Add turkey. Refrigerate for 48 hours, turning the turkey occasionally so it is evenly brined.

Fill pan of water smoker with water. Smoke-cook turkey for 6 to 8 hours, adding wood as necessary. Smaller birds will take less time.

Mike D. Adcock
Napton, MO

Spicy Kielbasa

1 lb. trimmed boneless venison or other
  big-game meat
1½ lbs. boneless fatty pork shoulder or butt
2 ice cubes, crushed
3 cloves garlic, minced or pressed
1 to 2 T. sweet paprika
1 T. coarse or kosher salt
1 T. coarse black pepper
2 tsp. crumbled dried marjoram leaves
1 tsp. crumbled dried savory leaves
1 tsp. ground allspice

In large bowl, combine all ingredients and mix very well. Grind through coarse grinding plate. Test for seasoning by frying a small patty; correct seasoning if necessary. Refrigerate sausage, uncovered, for 3 to 24 hours before cooking in order to develop its flavor.

For bulk sausage: Double-wrap and freeze no longer than 6 months.

For cased sausages: Prepare 2-inch-wide pork or beef casings and stuff (see Wild Boar and Venison Sausage, page 142, but do not blanch before freezing). Wrap well and freeze no longer than 6 months.

    This sausage goes well with caraway-seasoned sauerkraut and potatoes. For extra flavor, make the 2 ice cubes from beef stock instead of water.

Felicia Randall
Traverse City, MI

Jewish Garlic Sausage

2 lbs. boneless moose
2 medium onions, grated
2 eggs, beaten with 2 T cold water
1 large carrot, grated
8 to 10 cloves garlic, minced
¼ cup cold water
2 T. chopped fresh parsley
Salt and pepper
Fine matzo meal
Vegetable oil

Cube meat and grind through coarse plate. In large bowl, combine ground moose, onion and eggs and mix very well. Add carrot, garlic, water, parsley, and salt and pepper to taste; mix with your hands until well blended. Test for seasoning by frying a small patty; correct seasoning if necessary. Form into sausages about 3 inches long and ¾ inch in diameter. Roll sausages in matzo meal and fry in vegetable oil until cooked through and browned evenly.

    These are great on the breakfast table, and equally at home on the appetizer tray.

Andi Flanagan
Seward, AK

Jan's Spicy Salami

Foil-Baked Summer Sausage

Note: These basic instructions apply to all the recipes on this page.

In large bowl, combine all ingredients and mix very well with your hands. Divide mixture into 2 equal portions. Form each portion into a roll that is 2 to 3 inches in diameter. Wrap each roll individually in aluminum foil, shiny side in (facing the meat). Refrigerate for 24 hours. Poke holes in the bottom side of the foil and place on a rack that has been placed on a baking sheet, unless otherwise directed. Bake as directed. Cool completely and refrigerate.

Jan's Spicy Salami

2 lbs. ground venison
¾ cup cold beef broth
1 tsp. liquid smoke
3 T. Morton Tender Quick curing salt
2 cloves garlic, pressed or finely minced
2 T. paprika
1½ tsp. brown sugar
1½ tsp. mustard seed
1 tsp. fennel seed
½ tsp. onion juice
½ tsp. ground cayenne pepper, or to taste
¼ tsp. coarsely ground black pepper

Mix, form, wrap in foil and refrigerate as directed above. Bake at 325°F for 1½ hours.

For an attractive appetizer platter, roll the cold salami in chopped parsley, lemon pepper or other seasoned pepper blend, or mustard seeds before slicing. Serve with pumpernickel bread and thinly sliced red onions.

Jan Rose
Forest Lake, MN

Billy's Summer Sausage

1 lb. ground venison
1 lb. ground pork
1 cup cold water
½ tsp. liquid smoke
3 T. Morton Tender Quick curing salt
1 tsp. mustard seed
½ tsp. onion powder
¼ tsp. garlic powder
⅛ tsp. pepper

Mix, form, wrap in foil and refrigerate as directed above. Bake at 325°F for 1½ hours.

Billy Lansdown
Mountain View, MO

Babe's Peppercorn Salami

2 lbs. ground elk or other wild meat
3 T. Morton Tender Quick curing salt
½ tsp. whole peppercorns, or more to taste
½ tsp. ground pepper
½ tsp. mustard seed
½ tsp. garlic powder

Mix, form, wrap in foil and refrigerate as directed above. Place wrapped rolls in baking dish and add water to come halfway up the rolls. Bake at 350°F for 1 hour.

Babe Love
Loveland, CO

Peking Goose

Brine:

1½ cups cold water
1 cup soy sauce
½ cup sherry
1 (6-oz.) can pineapple juice
3 T. ketchup
2 T. brown sugar
1 small onion, minced
3 cloves garlic, minced

1 whole dressed Canada goose, preferably
   skin-on
Cherry wood chips or other wood chips
   for smoking
Bottled plum sauce
Hot cooked rice

In large pot, combine all brine ingredients, stirring to mix well. Add goose, and refrigerate overnight.

The next day, remove goose from brine and pat dry inside and out; discard brine. Hang goose in a dry, cool location for 4 hours, or until a glaze has formed on the outside of the goose; you may speed the process by directing a small electric fan at the hanging goose. The glaze is called a *pellicle*, and is important for retaining moisture in the meat during smoking.

When the outside of the goose has a nice glazed finish, place it on an oiled rack in a preheated electric smoker. Smoke-cook for 3 hours, using 2 pans of wood chips. Finish cooking goose in 325°F oven; this will take approximately 1 hour. Slice the goose and serve with plum sauce and rice. A stir-fry of zucchini and carrots, accented with sesame seeds, would be good with this dish.

Andi Flanagan
Seward, AK

Wild Game Polish Sausage

7 lbs. boneless venison, elk or antelope
3 lbs. bacon ends and pieces
1 quart cold water
2 cups powdered milk
3 large cloves garlic, minced
5 T. pickling/canning salt

2 T. Morton Tender Quick curing salt
2 T. ground black pepper
2 T. ground allspice
1 T. sugar
1½ tsp. crumbled dried marjoram leaves

Cut venison and bacon into cubes. Grind through ⅛-inch grinding plate. In large bowl, combine remaining ingredients, mixing well. Add ground meat and mix well by hand. Re-grind mixture through ⅛-inch grinding plate. Prepare 35mm to 38mm hog casings and stuff (see Wild Boar and Venison Sausage, page 142, but do not blanch). Sausages can then be smoked or frozen.

Dave Bezold
Sinclair, WY

Rabbit or Squirrel Breakfast Sausage

6 lbs. dressed rabbit or squirrel
2 tsp. salt
1½ tsp. rubbed sage
1¼ tsp. white pepper

¾ tsp. ground nutmeg
½ tsp. ground cinnamon
1 cup finely chopped peeled tart apple
2 T. vegetable oil

Bone rabbits. Cut meat into cubes and discard bones. In mixing bowl, combine rabbit meat, salt, sage, white pepper, nutmeg and cinnamon; mix well. Cover and refrigerate overnight. The next day, grind in meat grinder or process in food processor until coarsely ground, working with small batches. Stir in apple. Shape into 16 patties, each about 3 inches across. In large skillet, cook patties in oil over medium heat for 5 minutes on each side, or until sausage is browned and no longer pink inside.

James Happel
Denver, IA

Wild Boar & Venison Sausage

5 lbs. ground lean wild boar meat
5 lbs. ground venison
2 lbs. ground pork shoulder
1 cup paprika
1 cup sugar
½ to 1 cup salt (start with ½ cup)

¼ cup granulated garlic (garlic powder)
¼ cup hot red pepper flakes
¼ cup fennel seed
2 cups chopped fresh parsley
2 T. black pepper
1½ cups ice water

If you have a meat grinder, mix all ingredients in large mixing bowl and run through grinder again; if you don't have a grinder, simply mix by hand until mixture is thoroughly combined. Test for seasoning by frying a small patty; add additional salt if desired. Cover and refrigerate for 1 hour.

For bulk sausage: Portion into 1-pound packages, wrap with freezer paper, and freeze for later use.

For cased sausages: Prepare hog casings by rinsing, then thread casings onto stuffer horn. Load sausage mix into hopper and begin stuffing sausages, keeping enough pressure on the casings to form a firm sausage. Twist off sausages every 6 or 7 inches, and make each bundle of sausage 2½ to 3 pounds. The sausages can be frozen raw, or they can be blanched in boiling water for 15 minutes before freezing.

No matter how you finish the sausage, this is a great way to use up all your trimmings when you butcher your own game.

Michael Gordon
Venice, FL

Venison Kielbasa à la Butte

2 lbs. lean venison cubes
¼ lb. side pork
¼ lb. bacon
4 cloves garlic, minced
2 tsp. salt

2 tsp. crumbled dried marjoram leaves
1 tsp. sugar
1 tsp. freshly ground black pepper
½ cup bitter ale

Grind venison, salt pork and bacon together. Combine in large bowl with remaining ingredients, mix well and grind once more.

For bulk sausage: Double-wrap and freeze no longer than 6 months. Bulk sausage can be added to soups and stews, as well as shaped into patties or balls and fried, barbecued or broiled; cook to well-done.

For cased sausages: Stuff in hog casings (see Wild Boar and Venison Sausage, above, but do not blanch before freezing) and freeze no longer than 6 months. To prepare cased sausages, boil in water for 30 minutes, barbecue, or add to soups and stews for a delicious old-world flavor. Always cook to well-done.

Frank Bruno
Dubois, WY

Wild Boar & Venison Sausage

Poor Man's Venison Sausage

5 lbs. ground venison
5 T. Morton Tender Quick curing salt
2½ tsp. mustard seed
2½ tsp. garlic salt
2 tsp. pepper
1 tsp. celery seed
1 tsp. ground allspice
1 tsp. hickory smoked salt

In large bowl, combine all ingredients and mix very well with your hands. Cover and refrigerate for 3 days, kneading once each day.

On the fourth day, divide mixture into 4 equal portions. Form each portion into a roll that is approximately 2 inches in diameter. Place rolls on rack in broiling pan. Bake at 150°F for 4 hours. Turn rolls and continue baking for 6 hours longer (total 10 hours baking time), turning rolls every 2 hours. Cool on paper towels. Wrap in plastic wrap and refrigerate overnight before serving.

Ray Marlatt
Atlanta, MI

Mixed Game Breakfast Sausage

2 lbs. boneless, skinless mixed game (we use venison, pheasant and grouse)
1 lb. bacon, cut into 1-inch pieces
1 tsp. salt
½ tsp. freshly cracked black pepper
½ tsp. ground allspice
½ tsp. crumbled dried thyme leaves
4½ yards (approx.) small natural or collagen casings, *optional*

In large bowl, combine all ingredients except casings and mix very well. Chop one-third of the meat mixture finely in food processor. Transfer chopped meat to bowl and repeat with remaining meat mixture. Test for seasoning by frying a small patty; correct seasoning if necessary.

For cased sausages: Prepare natural casings as directed in Wild Boar and Venison Sausage, page 142; if using collagen casings, no preparation is necessary. Stuff as directed on page 142, twisting or tying into 4-inch links. Wrap well and freeze no longer than 6 months.

For bulk sausage: Shape sausage into patties. Layer patties with waxed paper, wrap well and freeze no longer than 6 months.

We like to sauté the links or patties in a little vegetable oil and serve them for breakfast, alongside pancakes and fresh berries.

Alex Kaniak
Sarasota, FL

Deer Leg Simply Smoked

1 venison hindquarter
1 (16-oz.) jar prepared mustard
Coarsely ground black pepper
Apple wood, hickory wood or mesquite
    chunks for smoking
1 lb. sliced bacon, approx.

Trim hindquarter of any bloodshot or ragged areas. Coat the hindquarter generously with mustard, using your hands; it's messy but is the best way to do this. Sprinkle with coarsely ground pepper. Place on oiled rack in water smoker; fill water pan with plain water. Smoke-cook for about 6 hours, adding wood as necessary and turning hindquarter occasionally. After 6 hours of smoke-cooking, wrap hindquarter in bacon strips and smoke-cook for 1 to 1½ hours longer. Slice thinly and serve.

Greg "Sparky" Sparkman
Gordonville, MO

Leftover Smoked Deer Leg

Leftover smoked hindquarter from recipe
    at left
Soy sauce
Sliced green bell peppers
1 (15¼-oz.) can mushrooms
1 (14¾-oz.) can mushroom gravy
Hot cooked rice

Cut smoked hindquarter into strips. In large skillet, heat venison strips with soy sauce and bell pepper strips until meat is browned. Add mushrooms and mushroom gravy; rinse gravy can with a full can of water and add to skillet. Simmer mixture to desired consistency. Serve over rice. Even your mother-in-law will like this dish.

Greg "Sparky" Sparkman
Gordonville, MO

Bear Sausage

30 lbs. ground bear meat
12 lbs. ground pork butt
3 lbs. slab bacon, ground
5 T. garlic salt
5 T. salt
2 T. plus 1½ tsp. ground black pepper
1 T. plus 2 tsp. hot red pepper flakes

In large bowl, combine all ingredients and mix very well. Test for seasoning by frying a small patty; correct seasoning if necessary. Fry in skillet for breakfast sausage, use on pizza, or make little meatballs for hors d'oeuvres.

Paul J. Woychik
Arcadia, WI

Dried Jerky

Dried Jerky with Variations

Note: These basic instructions apply to all of the recipes on pages 147 through 149. All recipes have been adjusted to use 2 pounds of boneless meat.

<u>Slicing the meat</u>: Trim meat of all silverskin, fat or gristle. Meat will be easier to slice if partially frozen. Slice meat to thickness recommended in individual recipe. For tender jerky, slice meat *across* the grain; for chewier jerky, slice meat *with* the grain.

<u>Marinating the meat</u>: Combine marinade ingredients in large nonaluminum bowl; a plastic ice cream pail also works well, as does a zipper-style plastic food storage bag. Add meat and stir to coat with marinade. Cover and refrigerate for time directed in individual recipe, stirring occasionally.

<u>Drying the meat</u>: Remove meat from marinade and pat dry; discard marinade. Arrange meat on racks as directed below, and process until meat is dry but not brittle.
- *To dry in dehydrator,* arrange meat in single layer on dehydrator trays; allow space between strips for air circulation. Process at 140°F to 150°F, rotating racks every hour or two.
- *To dry in oven,* arrange strips on finely spaced wire rack, allowing space between strips for air circulation; or, hang meat strips from oven racks. Prop oven door slightly open with small ball of foil. Set oven at 150°F or lowest setting, and bake until jerky is desired consistency.

Tangy-Sweet Jerky

3/8 cup cider vinegar
1/4 cup brown sugar
1/4 cup soy sauce
2 T. liquid smoke
1 T. plus 1 1/2 tsp. dried onion, or
    2 T. diced fresh onion
1 clove garlic, minced
1/4 tsp. hot red pepper flakes
1/4 tsp. black pepper
2 lbs. venison, sliced 1/8 to 3/16 inch thick

Follow basic instructions above, marinating at least 12 hours.

You may wish to include honey, corn syrup or molasses in the marinade for a sweeter flavor. For a spicier jerky, add ground cayenne pepper or jalapeño pepper to the marinade.

Bob Gross
Vincentown, NJ

Joe's Jerky

<u>Marinade:</u>
2/3 cup apple cider
1/3 cup soy sauce
2 T. plus 1 1/2 tsp. ketchup
1 T. salt
1 tsp. white pepper
1/2 tsp. ground ginger
1/2 tsp. ground cloves
1/2 tsp. onion powder
1/2 tsp. garlic powder

2 lbs. boneless venison, sliced approx.
    1/8 inch thick
2 tsp. ground cayenne pepper, *optional*

Combine marinade ingredients; cover and refrigerate overnight. After this, follow basic instructions above, marinating 1 to 3 days. Sprinkle meat with cayenne pepper before drying.

Joseph I. Chamberlain
Summerville, SC

Stanley's Teriyaki Venison Jerky

½ cup teriyaki sauce
2 tsp. liquid smoke
2 tsp. garlic pepper
1 tsp. onion powder
½ tsp. garlic powder
½ tsp. hot red pepper flakes
¼ tsp. Worcestershire sauce
2 lbs. venison, thinly sliced

Follow basic instructions on page 147, marinating at least 24 hours (longer if desired).

Stanley Martin
Frenchburg, KY

Whole-Muscle Jerky

2½ tsp. Morton Tender Quick curing salt
⅛ tsp. garlic powder
¼ tsp. onion powder
⅛ tsp. mace
¼ tsp. white pepper
¼ tsp. hot red pepper flakes or ground cayenne pepper
1 tsp. black pepper
Generous ¼ tsp. Season-All salt
1¼ tsp. liquid smoke
⅔ cup water
2 lbs. venison, thinly sliced

Follow basic instructions on page 147, marinating overnight.

Brenda Schultz
Steele, ND

David's Peppered Turkey Jerky

2 T. garlic salt
1 T. pepper
1 T. plus ¾ tsp. seasoned salt
1 T. plus 1½ tsp. sprinkle-on meat tenderizer
2 lbs. boneless, skinless wild turkey meat, sliced ¼ inch thick

This is a dry seasoning mix rather than a wet marinade, so the method is slightly different. Combine seasoning ingredients in gallon-sized plastic food storage bag; shake to mix. Add turkey strips and shake to coat. Arrange seasoned strips on racks and dry as described on page 147. Drying time will be 5 to 8 hours.

Tim Morgan
Dallas, TX

Deer Jerky with Taco Sauce

¼ cup soy sauce
1 T. Worcestershire sauce
1 T. taco sauce
1 tsp. liquid smoke
½ tsp. onion powder
¼ tsp. pepper
¼ tsp. garlic powder
2 dashes Tabasco sauce
2 lbs. venison, thinly sliced

Follow basic instructions on page 147, marinating for 24 hours.

William C. Smith
Callaway, VA

Keith's Venison Jerky

¼ cup soy sauce
¼ cup plus 1 T. brown sugar
2 T. Worcestershire sauce
1 T. A-1 steak sauce
1½ tsp. barbecue sauce
1 tsp. onion powder
½ tsp. garlic powder
½ tsp. mesquite-flavored seasoning salt
½ tsp. sprinkle-on meat tenderizer
¼ tsp. black pepper
¼ tsp. barbecue seasoning,
¼ tsp. liquid smoke
2 lbs. venison, thinly sliced

Follow basic instructions on page 147, marinating overnight.

D. Keith Ward
Marshall, VA

As-You-Like-It Venison Jerky

1 cup cider vinegar
3 T. Worcestershire sauce
2 T. soy sauce
1 T. Heinz 57 sauce
1 T. A-1 steak sauce
2 tsp. Tabasco sauce
1 tsp. sea salt
½ tsp. garlic powder
½ tsp. ground cayenne pepper
¼ tsp. dry mustard
2 lbs. venison, sliced ¼ inch thick

Follow basic instructions on page 147, marinating for 24 hours. For spicier jerky, sprinkle meat with additional cayenne pepper after arranging on racks; or sprinkle any seasoning you like on the meat before drying.

Sherman Morton
Centerville, GA

No-Salt Jerky

1½ cups apple cider
⅜ cup cider vinegar
⅜ cup brown sugar
2 T. chopped onion
1½ tsp. garlic powder
Crystal hot sauce or Tabasco sauce to taste,
    optional
2 lbs. venison, sliced ⅛ to 3/16 inch thick

Follow basic instructions on page 147, marinating at least 12 hours; if marinade does not cover meat, add cold water as needed.

Bob Gross
Vincentown, NJ

Sweet Italian Sausage

1 lb. lean boneless venison
1 lb. boneless fatty pork shoulder or butt
1 to 2 tsp. fennel seed
1 tsp. salt
1 tsp. sugar
½ tsp. garlic powder
½ tsp. lemon pepper
½ tsp. paprika
¼ tsp. celery salt
¼ tsp. rubbed sage
⅛ tsp. ground cayenne pepper
1 T. soy sauce
1 tsp. Worcestershire sauce

Cut venison and pork into ¾-inch cubes. In small bowl, mix remaining ingredients except soy sauce and Worcestershire sauce. Sprinkle mixed seasonings over meat and toss to coat. Sprinkle soy sauce and Worcestershire sauce over seasoned meat, tossing to coat. Cover and refrigerate for 8 hours, or overnight.

The next day, grind seasoned meat through medium plate of meat grinder. Test for seasoning by frying a small patty; correct seasoning if necessary. Use sausage for pizza topping, to make meatballs for spaghetti, or as breakfast patties. Sausage also freezes well.

Felicia Randall
Traverse City, MI

Venison Country Sausage

10 lbs. ground venison
¾ cup brown sugar
¼ cup canning/pickling salt
3 T. fennel seed
2 tsp. nutmeg
2 tsp. hot red pepper flakes or
    ground cayenne pepper
2 tsp. ground ginger
½ cup cold water, approx.

In large bowl, combine all ingredients except water and mix very well. Add water as needed if mixture is dry. Test for seasoning by frying a small patty; correct seasoning if necessary.

For cased sausages: Prepare natural casings as directed in Wild Boar and Venison Sausage, page 142; if using collagen casings, no preparation is necessary. Stuff as directed on page 142, twisting or tying into 4-inch links. Wrap well and freeze no longer than 6 months.

For bulk sausage: Shape sausage into patties. Layer patties with waxed paper, wrap well and freeze no longer than 6 months.

Aden D. Miller
Windsor, OH

Smoked Duck Breasts with Sauerkraut

Boneless, skinless breast filets from 4 ducks
1/4 cup vegetable oil
1/4 cup soy sauce
2 T. ketchup
1 T. red wine vinegar
1 small onion, chopped
3 cloves garlic, chopped

Cherry or apple wood shavings for smoking
2 tart apples, cored and sliced
2-quart bag refrigerated sauerkraut,
  rinsed and drained
1 cup chicken broth
1 tsp. Dijon-style mustard

In 13×9×2-inch baking dish, arrange duck breast filets in single layer. Combine oil, soy sauce, ketchup, vinegar, onion and garlic in glass jar. Cover tightly and shake to blend. Pour mixture over duck breasts. Cover dish with plastic wrap and refrigerate overnight.

The next day, drain duck breasts, discarding marinade. Place duck breasts on rack of cold smoker, and cold-smoke for 2 or 3 hours, adding wood shavings once per hour. When duck breasts have smoked for 2 or 3 hours, transfer to lightly greased 13×9×2-inch baking dish. Top with apple slices; spread sauerkraut evenly over apples. Blend together chicken broth and mustard; pour around duck breasts. Cover and bake at 300°F for 1 to 1¼ hours, or until duck breasts are desired doneness.

Teresa Marrone
Minneapolis, MN

Baked Stuffed Acorn Squash

2 lbs. Italian-style game sausage, uncased
½ cup Italian-seasoned bread crumbs
2 eggs, beaten
1 to 2 T. milk
½ tsp. minced garlic
½ tsp. black pepper

¼ tsp. hot red pepper flakes, *optional*
2 acorn squash, split into halves, seeds
    and pulpy core removed
¼ cup olive oil
Salt and pepper

In mixing bowl, combine sausage, bread crumbs, eggs, milk, garlic, black pepper, and red pepper. Mix well with your hands. Divide mixture into fourths, and form each into a ball. Place a sausage ball into each of the squash cavities; pat down gently. Coat each with a tablespoon of the olive oil, and salt and pepper to taste. Arrange squash, cut-side up, in a baking dish. Fill dish a third of the way up with water, and cover dish with foil. Bake at 325°F for 1 hour.

David G. Petta
Albion, NY

Venison Pan Sausage Bread

1 (1-lb.) loaf frozen bread dough
1 lb. venison sausage, any variety, uncased
1 medium green bell pepper, chopped
1 medium onion, chopped
Vegetable cooking spray

1 cup shredded cheddar cheese
1 cup shredded Monterey Jack or
    mozzarella cheese
1 egg, beaten
Picante sauce for serving

Thaw bread and let rise according to package directions. When bread is almost done rising, cook sausage, bell pepper and onion in large skillet over medium heat until sausage is browned and vegetables are tender, stirring to break up meat. Drain and discard excess grease; set aside.

Spray baking sheet with vegetable cooking spray. Roll out bread dough in rectangular shape and place on baking sheet. Spread half the sausage mixture over the dough, keeping the edges clear. Sprinkle with half of each of the cheeses. Repeat with remaining sausage and cheeses. Gently brush cold water on edges of bread dough. Fold dough at top, and then fold ends to completely enclose sausage and cheese. Brush bread roll with beaten egg. Bake at 375°F for 20 minutes. Slice and serve with your favorite picante sauce. Our hunters really enjoy this.

Mary Greider
Houston, TX

Baked Stuffed Acorn Squash

Pickled Venison Polish Sausage

5 to 6 lbs. venison Polish sausage links
1 tsp. sugar
1 tsp. crumbled dried thyme leaves
1 tsp. garlic powder
1 tsp. hot red pepper flakes
1 tsp. minced onion
1 tsp. onion salt
1 tsp. garlic salt
1 tsp. celery salt
2 T. crumbled dried oregano leaves
Cold water
Red wine vinegar

Fill a wide-mouth glass gallon jug with 4- to 6-inch lengths of venison Polish sausage. Sprinkle the top with sugar, thyme, garlic powder, red pepper, onion, onion salt, garlic salt and celery salt. Sprinkle oregano over other seasonings. Fill jug one-quarter full with cold water, then fill completely with wine vinegar. Cover jar and refrigerate at least a week; the longer it sits, the better it will taste.

The most difficult part of this recipe is finding a butcher to make you good Polish sausage from your venison. The size, texture and seasoning should be as similar as possible to Hillshire Farms' Polish sausage. Hard-boiled eggs may be pickled in the same recipe, omitting the oregano and thyme.

Fred Hungerford
Oneonta, NY

Game Sausage in Sauce

2 to 3 lbs. Italian-style game sausage links
2 T. olive oil
4 cloves garlic, minced
2 (28-oz.) cans tomato purée
Cold water to fill 28-oz. can
3 T. chopped fresh parsley
2 T. chopped fresh basil leaves
1½ tsp. chopped fresh oregano leaves
4 bay leaves
Salt and pepper to taste

Cut sausage into 2-inch lengths. In large skillet, brown sausage pieces in olive oil over medium heat. Add garlic and sauté for about a minute; be careful to prevent the garlic from browning. Transfer sausage and garlic mixture to slow cooker. Add remaining ingredients to slow cooker. Cover and cook on low for about 6 hours. This makes a great hors d'oeuvre for a party, or serve it over rice or pasta for a main course.

David G. Petta
Albion, NY

Venison Sausage Balls

1 lb. spicy venison sausage, uncased
1 small onion, chopped
1 (8-oz.) pkg. shredded cheddar cheese
3 cups buttermilk baking mix such as Bisquick

Brown sausage and onion in skillet, stirring to break up meat. Combine in large bowl with remaining ingredients. Form into 1-inch balls and place on greased cookie sheet. Bake at 350°F for 30 minutes. Transfer balls to slow cooker; cover and keep warm on low heat. Serve as appetizer.

Jim Kilgore
Bellevue, KY

Wild Sausage & Vegetable Dinner

1 lb. venison or wild hog sausage links
3 medium baking potatoes, cut into 1/3-inch thick slices crosswise
1 bell pepper, cut into squares
3 medium carrots, cut into 3 x 1/2-inch strips
1 medium head cabbage, cored and quartered
1 onion, quartered
Salt and pepper
1 cup water
1/2 cup red table wine

Cut sausage diagonally into 1/2-inch-thick slices. Layer potatoes, sausage, bell pepper, carrots, cabbage and onion in order listed in Dutch oven or large electric skillet, sprinkling each layer with salt and pepper. Add water and wine. Heat to boiling; reduce heat and cover. Simmer for 30 to 45 minutes, or until vegetables are tender, adding additional water if needed.

Joe Barbara
Fort Worth, TX

Potato-Venison Sausage Soup

1/2 lb. venison sausage, uncased
4 cups grated potatoes
1 large onion, chopped
1 (14 1/2-oz.) can chicken broth
2 cups water
1 (10 3/4-oz.) can cream of celery soup
1 (10 3/4-oz.) can cream of chicken soup
2 cups milk
1 1/2 tsp. dried dill weed, *optional*
Shredded cheddar cheese for garnish

In Dutch oven, brown sausage over medium heat, stirring to break up. Drain and discard excess grease. Add potatoes, onion, chicken broth and water; heat to boiling. Cover and reduce heat; simmer for 30 minutes. Add cream soups, milk and dill, stirring to blend. Cook over medium heat, stirring often, until thoroughly heated. Garnish with shredded cheddar cheese.

Richard M. Mann
Ada, OK

INDEX

HUNTING REWARDS